DAVID W. MELBER

THE MAKING OF A MESSIAH

INFLUENCES ON JESUS' CHILDHOOD AND YOUTH

A NOVEL

ALPHA OMEGA PUBLISHERS

Library of Congress Cataloging-in-Publication Data

Melber, David W.
The Making of a Messiah: Influences on Jesus' Childhood and Youth

ISBN:1-59330-681-4

Library of Congress Control Number: 2010912842
Library of Congress Cataloging-in-Publication Data
The Making of a Messiah

Copyright © David W. Melber
Alpha Omega Publishing Company
dwmelber@aol.com

All rights reserved.
Reprint or reproduction, even partially, in all form such as microfilm, xerography, microfiche, microcard, and offset strictly prohibited.

Printed in the United States

Cover Photo:

For
Ann
The quintessence of
Christian *agape*
and courage

TABLE OF CONTENTS

PREFACE	vii
INTRODUCTION	ix
CAST	xiii
CHAPTER 1 - A SUSPICIOUS BIRTH	1
CHAPTER 2 - INTERNATIONAL POLITICS INTERVENES	9
CHAPTER 3 - A CHAOTIC INFANCY	15
CHAPTER 4 - HISTORY LEADING TO HEROD	19
CHAPTER 5 - UNLIKELY FOREIGN HONORS	23
CHAPTER 6 - A NEW LIFE	31
CHAPTER 7 - CHILD GROWS IN WISDOM AND STATURE	45
CHAPTER 8 - THE RETURN	51
CHAPTER 9 - JOSHUA'S EDUCATION CONTINUES	57
CHAPTER 10 - RABBINICAL INFLUENCE	67
CHAPTER 11 - OTHER INFLUENCES ON JOSHUA	75
CHAPTER 12 - PREPARATION FOR MINISTRY	87
CHAPTER 13 - INTENSIVE EDUCATION	99
CHAPTER 14 - MINISTRY OF JOHN THE BAPTIZER	113
CHAPTER 15 - INITIATION FOR THE MINISTRY	123
EPILOGUE	135
BIBLIOGRAPHY	139

PREFACE

The English transliteration of Jesus' name in Hebrew is *Joshua* (*Yeshua* is actually closer. But then transliterations from one language to another are rarely exact). That is probably what his parents and friends called him. However, when he began to come into contact with Hellenized Jews and Gentiles, he may have used the Greek name of *Jesus*. That is the name in English translations of the Greek ίηοῦς. So in his earlier years, I am calling him Joshua. The name Jesus is used in most of his ministry. The same is true of other people. The English *Mary* will be *Miriam*. The English transliteration of the Aramaic term for "son of" will be *bar*. In a few instances the transliteration of the Hebrew term *ben* will be used for "son of." The English transliteration of the Aramaic term "daughter of" is *bat*.

The English transliteration of the Hebrew name for the covenant God's name is *Yahweh* (in the King James Version of the Older Testament, it was spelled LORD—all capitals). However, after a tragic incident in the use of God's names (Lev. 24:11-16), Israelites were afraid to say Yahweh's name for fear of using it in vain. Therefore, when they needed to speak the Name, they substituted the name *Adonai*. In the book, when the name is spoken, the name *Adonai* will be used. When the Hebrew Bible is quoted in the narration of the story, the name *Yahweh* will be used.

Most Biblical passages are from the New International Version (NIV), copyright © 1973, 1978, 1984 by *Biblica*, or my adaptation thereof. The Bibliography has a list of the books of which I am conscious of using significantly. Any other incidence is simply from my head of sixty five years of reading.

When the author of a book lists those he is grateful to for help in the final production, it often sounds like an ingenuous Academy

Award acceptance speech. But when one writes a book, it becomes clearer just how true those expressions of appreciation are.

I am not one who can keep a lot of balls in the air. When I have a project, the rest of the world gets blocked out. My wife, Ann, has put up with a great deal of neglect during this project with grace and patience. A fellow senior softball player and former member of the editorial staff of *First Army Voice*, Jack Wilkenson, in his copy editing and content editing, caught so many grammatical and structural "booboos" that it is embarrassing to call the book mine. I am very thankful for Dr. Thom Prentice, retired literature professor at Texas State University, who not only reviewed my book from a literary perspective, but gave me major encouragement when I turned over to him a very early draft of the book. After beginning work on editing the book, physical limitations due to cancer and its treatments, required him to stop his editing. When I asked Rev. Ray Tiemann, bishop of the Southwestern Texas Synod of the Evangelical Lutheran Church in America; Rev. Lori Ruge-Jones; and Dr. Phil Ruge-Jones for a recommendation of whom to ask to review the book from a historical and theological point of view, they all agreed that there was only one person for the job – Dr. Norman Beck, Poehlmann Professor of Theology and Classical Languages at Texas Lutheran University. Their insight was great. I am so thankful to Dr. Beck, who did a magnificent job of editing and sharing insights.

INTRODUCTION

Our contexts help make us who we are and help explain our way of thinking and how we respond to occurrences in the world around us. Unless we understand a person's context, we don't understand a person's actions. Our background provides our mental constructs. Ideology is thinking that must be defended. Ideology never questions its way of thinking. It never looks for the truth, because it already believes it knows the truth. Ideology defends itself in such a way that it even fools itself.

We all live within contexts. They have an extremely significant influence on what we become. When one reads a text without knowing the context, s/he does not usually understand what the text means. Even the ideas and ideals we carry around in our heads are part of the context of our lives and explain what we do and even what we see.

The way people are usually taught about Jesus makes him an ethereal, unreal person. Many Christians never progress past their children's Sunday school understanding of Jesus. And because of that, Jesus is often not meaningful to such people outside a funny-looking building with a steeple. They learn a little about some of Paul's theology about Jesus and become satisfied that if they just "believe in Jesus," they can say "kings-ex" to hell and hello to heaven, whatever those might be. Jesus becomes a teacher of some nice, tame ideals that are irrelevant in a world of Wall Street, K Street, and Main Street. He ceases to be the one who claimed to usher in the Kingdom of God with revolutionary teachings that turn the world up-side down. Thus he is often ignored in real-life by those who claim him.

During the Middle Ages, Jesus became so ethereal that he was pictured as a remote king, wearing a prestigious crown, an unapproachable figure. Therefore, Mary became the savior, one with whom they could personally identify, who might put in a good word for them with her son-king. After all, who would have more influenced on the remote figure than his mom?

Some of our most beloved Christmas carols make Jesus unreal. In the song *Away in A Manger,* expressions such as "no crying he makes" and "look down from the sky" turn the baby into something unreal. But Jesus was a real person. As a baby, he did cry, he did dirty his diapers. He had to learn the Scriptures like any other Jewish boy. He had to learn his times tables. Like other children, his parents would have been his primary teachers by their words and by their modeling of what a good Jew was like.

The way he turned out, it seems that his parents were a good influence on him. But there were other teachers. We do not know who they were. His early formal education was probably received under the local Nazareth rabbi. Some scholars believe that Jesus may have studied at the Essene community of Qumran (the community of the Dead Sea Scrolls). There are some similarities in Jesus' teaching and theirs, but there are also major differences. They had a baptismal type rite. They also had a eucharistic type meal of bread and wine. But contrary to the humility of Jesus, the members of the Qumran community were quite self-righteous. And contrary to the Qumran community, Jesus was open to Gentiles as well as all Jews.

Others believe that John the Baptizer, a cousin of Jesus, may have been a part of that Essene community for a while and that Jesus may have been a disciple of John, but later developed his own theology and ethic. Both John and Jesus proclaimed the advent of "the kingdom of Adonai." But as sainted Rev. Vance Daniels liked to say, when John proclaimed it, he meant "it is five minutes until midnight." When Jesus proclaimed it, he meant "it is midnight," that is, "the kingdom is here."

This book is a novel, not a history. But neither are the Four Gospels. My book is an attempt, based on the Gospels, as well as apocrypha, and pseudepigraphical writings (second century writings that tried to fill in blanks in Jesus' childhood that are not in the Scriptural canon), historical books about Jesus' life, books on human development, and my own imagination. As a Christian, I would like to see this book motivate people to go back to the Gospels, to learn what Jesus taught, to take what he taught seriously, to follow his teaching, and thereby make the world a more humane place in which to live. For, after all, faith is not merely cognitive assent to a set of propositions. It is not an ecstatic feeling of "God's presence." It is not keeping a set of laws. It is not regularity at congregational worship. It is a relationship with God that is expressed in doing God's will with regard to God's creation.

David W. Melber

August 2010

CAST

Joshua/Jesus bar Joseph – the Messiah
Joseph bar Jakov – Father of the Messiah
Miriam bat Joachim – Mother of the Messiah
Zechariah – Father of John the Baptizer
Elizabeth – Mother of John the Baptizer
John bar Zechariah, the Baptizer – Joshua's cousin and mentor
Baltasar, Caspar, Melchior, Aleister, and Abashar – magi from Parthia
Herod the Great bar Antipater– King of Israel from 40 to 4 BCE
Farik – Egyptian carpenter in Tanis, who employed Joseph
James, Joseph, Judah, and Simon bar Joseph – brothers of Joshua
Farouk – an Egyptian boyhood friend of Joshua
Hillel – greatest Jewish rabbi of all time, a mentor of Joshua

CHAPTER 1

A SUSPICIOUS BIRTH

A Suspicious Pregnancy

Miriam thanked Yahweh for her husband, Joseph bar Jakov. She had been unmarried and pregnant. In an honor-shame society like theirs, Joseph and his family would personally be offended by her premature pregnancy. They could require that she be stoned to death. But Joseph never had leaned in the direction of vindictiveness. He had not seen Miriam's face as an adult. Joseph had known Miriam in the days when she was young enough not to wear a veil. He was seventeen years older than Miriam. He had not seen her face recently.

Her parents, Joachim and Anna, had lived for twenty years without children. After years of humiliation, including snide comments by the High Priest about her barrenness, Joachim and Anna had a daughter. Rumor had it that, like Samuel's birth to Hannah, this child was brought forth by promise, and the child had been committed to serving Yahweh in the temple. After three years' weaning, she was taken to the temple and dedicated to serve Yahweh and receive an education. In addition to praying, one of her duties was the weaving of purple cloth.

Only recently, at age fourteen, she had had her first menstrual period and had donned a veil as a young woman, "now of a proper maturity for marriage." And in accordance with her wishes, the High Priest in Jerusalem had gone into the Holy of Holies to consult Yahweh, and heard from the Ark of the Covenant that she should be a virgin, yet have a child that fulfilled Isaiah's prophecy.

Joseph's parents were both dead and at thirty-one he was well past the time to begin thinking about marriage. All Joseph ever saw of Miriam was her dark-brown (almost black), piercing and compassionate-looking eyes. He had recently negotiated with Miriam's family to marry her. A comparatively small dowry was agreed on. The wedding date was set for the late spring.

However, there was a fly in the ointment. Miriam had become pregnant and within three months of their betrothal, it was obvious. But in the month of Quintilis (Elul in the Jewish calendar), during a sweltering hot summer, Miriam had a dream of the angel Gabriel, who said, "Hello, Miriam! You are highly favored. The Lord is with you." In her sleep she was troubled, tossed and turned, and whimpered.

But the angel said, "Do not be afraid, Miriam. You have found favor with Yahweh. You will be with child and give birth to a son, and you are to give him the name Joshua. He will be great and will be called the Son of the Most High. Yahweh God will give him the throne of his father David, and he will reign over the house of Jacob forever." Even in her dream state, there was an in incredulity to this statement. "How can this be, since I am a virgin?" she protested in her dream.

"The Holy Spirit will come upon you and the power of the Most High will overshadow you. So the holy one to be born will be called the son of Yahweh. Even your relative Elizabeth is going to have a child in her old age, and she who was said to be barren is in her sixth month. For nothing is impossible with Yahweh."

In her dream state, Miriam answered, "I am Adonai's (even in her dream state she could not bring herself to say the sacred name "Yahweh") servant. May it be to me as you have said." She awoke startled.

"So," she thought to herself, "this was no physical act. It was Adonai's doing." But what would Joseph think?

Joseph had been away, building a house in Sepphoris. When he returned, he could not believe what he saw. His beloved Miriam was pregnant. In his anguish he demanded to know who the father was. She broke into tears and swore to him that she didn't know how she had gotten pregnant. She swore to him that she had not had intercourse with anyone.

Joseph's Reaction

Joseph had no idea what to do. If he concealed her "crime," he would be guilty of defiling Yahweh's Torah. But if he reported her condition and her pregnancy actually was miraculous, he would be guilty of the death of an innocent person. He couldn't bear to exercise the full weight of the Torah on Miriam. Gossip of that nature spread like wildfire in Nazareth, but so far she had not been out in public and the family had informed only Joseph. So Joseph had determined to withdraw from the marriage contract and seek a suitable bride.

Miriam asked her sister, Deborah, to solicit Joseph to see her. Joseph responded positively and expected Miriam to beg his forgiveness and for her life. They were chaperoned, but at a far enough distance that the conversation could not be heard. Joseph was startled when she told him her story. She begged him to believe her. She reminded him of the miracles that were recorded in the Torah and the Prophets.

"But that was in the days of the prophets," Joseph protested. "Do you want me to believe that such things still happen?"

"I know," pleaded Miriam, "but that is what the angel told me in my dream."

Joseph was incredulous, but promised her that he would pray about the matter. He wanted so much to believe Miriam. His heart ached for her. If only her story could be true. He went home and prayed for Yahweh to give him direction, a sign. If such a miracle could occur, surely a sign could be given.

But in his broken-hearted state, he had trouble sleeping. In a dream he saw an angel that said, "Joseph, son of David, do not be afraid to take Miriam home as your wife, because what is conceived in her is from the Holy Spirit. She will give birth to a son, and you are to give him the name Joshua, because he will save his people from their sins."

Joseph woke with a start. Confused and upset, he could not eat. In times of crises, he often turned to the Psalms, which his parents had taught him and which he had had to memorize at the yeshiva school as a child. But none gave him comfort.

Joseph was a successful carpenter. He was not affluent, but neither was he as poor as many of his neighbors. Joseph was acquainted with some of the affluent people in Nazareth. Chaim bar Judah, a successful merchant in the Nazareth market, had often brought his business to Joseph. Recently Joseph had built an expensive acacia couch for Chaim.

Chaim had commissioned his own private copy of the prophet Isaiah. He had offered to let Joseph read it any time he wanted. Joseph had gratefully accepted the offer and had often memorized sections of the scroll. But there was a part that he vaguely remembered regarding the birth of a child who would have the name Immanuel, "God is with us." He needed guidance from Yahweh's prophet. So he rushed to the market. Chaim had several stalls in which members of his family worked.

"Tirza," Joseph asked, "where is your father?"

"He has gone to negotiate with Nathaniel, the fisherman from Capernaum. But any time Nathaniel has his sons, Simon and Andrew along, you can be sure that my father will be delayed."

"Thank you. I will be back later. You can tell him, I would like to have a little time to read his Isaiah scroll."

As she was about to answer, Joseph heard his name called. "Joseph, my brother."

As Joseph turned, he saw Chaim. With him was a man with whom he was slightly acquainted, Nathaniel and his two sons.

"Joseph, Nathaniel and I have just made a deal. We are going to celebrate. Would you join us?"

Yes. I would be glad to."

"Joseph, you know Nathaniel bar Shallum, don't you?" suggested Chaim.

"Oh, yes. We have met. Shalom chaverim Nathaniel."

"Shalom aleichem, Joseph. It has been a long time since I have seen you. I am glad you will join us," Nathaniel said enthusiastically. "And these are my sons, Simon and Andrew. Simon is four and Andrew is three. They have already been out on the boat with me several times. Simon is learning quite quickly how to fish. Andrew still just likes to play with live fish. But in a few years they will begin to take over the boat for me and become great fishermen."

"I'm sure you are right," affirmed Joseph. "Hello, boys. Will you someday take over the boat for your father?"

Simon nodded sheepishly. Andrew was in another world, the world of smells and sights in the market.

They made their way to Chaim's home, a large Roman style villa, with rooms around a large courtyard. The meal was a happy occasion. Almost all people in the eastern Roman Empire, regardless of their ethnic background, like to share meals with guests. Eating at Chaim's home was particularly enjoyable because he could afford the best wines and foods that were too expensive for most Jews. Besides bread, olive oil, and water and wine, he provided pomegranates, grapes, and lamb. It would be a long and leisurely meal.

As the boys played, the men talked about their futures and what they would have to leave to their sons. Joseph listened intently, with a tinge of ache in his heart. His prospect of such a thing had been turned upon its head. Finally, his worst fears were realized.

"What about you Joseph? When will you be taking Miriam into your home? You need to get started on raising a son."

"I am not sure right now. It may be a while." That is all he felt like saying.

"Come now, Joseph," joked Nathaniel, "you're not getting any younger. You need to get started passing on those good traits of a descendent of King David."

"I still have time. I have many things to consider." He wished he could unburden his heart, but that was all he could bring himself to say.

"What is to consider?" teased Chaim. "You are doing well in your carpentry shop. You need a son. You have Miriam, who is ready for child-bearing. It's time."

"Yes, I know you are right. It will not be long. But . . . ."

By now his insides were churning. He wished he could unburden his heart to his good friend, Chaim, but could not. He was afraid of what Chaim would think. He didn't want public humiliation. Nor did he want what could happen to Miriam. Her family might insist on her punishment, because pregnancy would be a humiliation to their honor not to do so.

As Joseph could see the fellowship was about to break up, he broached the subject of reading Isaiah.

"Of course. I must get back to the market. My wife is coming also, so you may stay and read," Chaim assured him.

"I cannot," responded Joseph. "Ahaziah, my apprentice, is by himself. I must get back."

"Well then, Joseph, you are my friend. Take the scroll home, read it tonight, and bring it back tomorrow or the next day. Or bring it to me on the Sabbath at the synagogue."

"I could not do that. It is too expensive."

No one would ever be so rude as to immediately accept a gift or favor, without first protesting that it is too great, no matter how fervently he wanted it. "Do not offend me by refusing my generosity toward you."

The negotiation goes on. "But what if, Adonai forbid, it should be damaged?"

"Adonai will preserve it," Chaim assured him.

"I will gratefully take it and with the blessing of Adonai on you. I will bring it back tomorrow," Joseph promised.

Joseph's New Perspective

That night Joseph pored over the scroll until he came to the story of the reign of Ahaz, king of Judah, over seven hundred years before. King Rezin of Aram had come from Damascus and King Pekah of Israel had left Samaria and attacked Jerusalem. Ahaz and his people were "shaken as the trees of the forest are shaken by the wind." Isaiah met with Ahaz at the end of the aqueduct of the

Upper Pool. He assured Ahaz that he should not fear, making fun of Rezin and Pekah, referring to them as "two smoldering stubs of firewood." To assure Ahaz, Isaiah had challenged Ahaz to ask for a sign from Yahweh.

With false piety, Ahaz responded, "I will not ask; I will not test Adonai." "Adonai" was the term they used as a substitute for "Yahweh," so that they would not accidentally use Yahweh's name in vain.

Angrily, Isaiah responded, "Adonai will give you a sign anyway. A young woman would bear a son called Immanuel, which means 'God is with us,' and before that son is old enough to be able to discern right from wrong, Assyria will come and destroy both Aram and Israel. And Assyria will lay waste to Judah also." And Isaiah's wife conceived a son, Maher-Shalal-Hash-Baz, which in Hebrew means "quick to the plunder, swift to the spoil."

Isaiah's prophecy was addressed to someone named "Immanuel." But the prophecy ends by assuring the reader that the nations that attack Judah will not prevail, because *Immanuel* ("God is with us").

As he read, Joseph thought the Hebrew word "almah," which means "a young unmarried woman," can also be interpreted to mean "a virgin." And in the dream, the angel said that the child's name would be "Joshua," which means "savior," because he will save his people from their sins. Who else could save the people from their sins, but "God with us." For Joseph, the prophecy must refer to the child in Miriam's womb. He concluded that she had not had illicit sex with anyone or had been raped. It must have been a miraculous birth like that of Isaac and Samuel. His doubts about Miriam were allayed.

Miriam's family had offered Joseph compensation for the dishonor that she had perpetrated on him with her pregnancy. Although he had considered it before, he could no longer think of such a thing. They had the marriage consummated with the marriage feast in a week. But there was another fly in the ointment,

Annas the scribe. He happened to spy Miriam and saw that she was pregnant. He went to the priest and complained that Joseph had committed a "notorious crime" by getting a virgin pregnant and then marrying her privately to hide what had been done.

So Miriam and Joseph were brought to trial. Both Miriam and Joseph denied that they had had sexual relations. Both were given a trial by ordeal. Originally, it was a trial given to a woman whose husband suspected her of adultery. She swore an oath that she was innocent, was given water with the blood-soaked dirt from the tabernacle floor. If she were guilty her stomach would swell and her thighs would wither. If she was innocent, nothing would happen. Over time the trial by ordeal was also applied to men who were suspect. Joseph and Miriam survived the trial, so the priest exonerated them.

Therefore, the marriage feast was arranged. After three days of feasting, Joseph took her into his home in the month of Febriarois (Shevat in the Jewish calendar). But that night none of the usual formalities were exercised; no family representatives made sure the marriage was consummated. Joseph did not have intercourse with Miriam until after the birth of her son and the appropriate time of cleansing after the birth as prescribed in the Torah of Moses.

CHAPTER 2
INTERNATIONAL POLITICS INTERVENES

Destination Bethlehem

Before the ordeal, the community temporarily shunned the couple. But once they survived the ordeal, the community was excited. It would be only a short time before Miriam would deliver. However, there was grist for considerable good-natured humor by those who did not buy into the sexless pregnancy story.

But there were clouds on the horizon called Rome. The emperor, Octavian of the household of Caesar, had been given the title Augustus by the Senate. He needed additional taxes to carry out his massive building programs during his twenty-five years reign. He later bragged regarding his building program that he had found Rome bricks and had left it marble. But first the population of his empire had to be enrolled in order to tax them more effectively. Rather than carrying out the census on people where they lived, descendents of David had to return to their ancestral homes to enroll. This made for an extraordinary hardship on many people, but for some unknown reason, Herod, administered the tax that way on Jews in his realm.

So in early Abib (Martium in the Julian calendar), Joseph began the arduous journey from Nazareth to Bethlehem. For Joseph by himself, it would not be that difficult. But the circumstances were the circumstances. Mary was in the eighth month of her pregnancy. The journey would be arduous for her, but Joseph wanted her with him. They assumed that they would be back in Nazareth before the child was born, but one never knows.

As the crow flies, the distance from Nazareth to Bethlehem is about eighty miles. But for many Jews, the trip to Bethlehem would be much longer. To get to Judah from Galilee, one would have to travel through Samaria. Many Jews refused to lay foot on Samaritan soil. The hatred between Samaritans and Jews was intense. So a solitary Jewish traveler in Samaria faced the risk of being attacked, or of being refused lodging or food. Therefore, many Jews would travel east from Nazareth south of Mt. Tabor, cross the Jordan River, go south along the Kings Highway through the Decapolis and Perea, cross the Jordan River again at Jericho, and proceed southwest to Bethlehem, adding about thirty-five to forty miles to the trip. But if they traveled directly through Samaria, defiling their feet, they usually traveled in caravans, which was safer than traveling alone. And the company made the trip more enjoyable.

The Decapolis was primarily Roman. Rome had given free land in the Decapolis to retired Roman soldiers. The Decapolis was a defensive shield against Rome's rival, Parthia, in the east.

Walking, with a donkey carrying his supplies, Joseph could make about twenty miles per day, and therefore arrive in Bethlehem in about four days. But Miriam was in the late stage of her pregnancy. So Joseph saddled a donkey with a great deal of padding on the saddle and Miriam rode it. They traveled the direct route. Joseph had never been inclined toward ethnic hatred. And in recent years, due to the close scrutiny of the Roman Legions, the *Pax Romana* had made traveling considerably safer.

Nevertheless, Joseph tried to stay with caravans, especially in the evening and at night. Unfortunately, because of Miriam's condition, they could not stay up with them. Due to the census, there were more caravans than usual. Joseph often slowed down in the afternoon in hopes that a caravan would catch up with them.

Fortunately for Miriam, the spring was mild and it was overcast at nights so that the heat was trapped and the nights were relatively warm. They could not have asked for better conditions for her. After seven days, they arrived in Bethlehem. It had not changed much since Joseph had been there to visit relatives five years before. He had not gone there often since his parents had died.

Because there were so many people in Bethlehem at that time, and the place where caravaners generally spent the night was very crowded, there was no room left in the sleeping area. Nor was there room in the homes of any of Joseph's distant relatives. On the second night after their arrival on Martius (Nissan) 21, 5 BCE*, the unexpected happened. Miriam went into labor. One of Joseph's second cousins, Benjamin bar David, prevailed on the local innkeeper, who still had no room for another guest in the inn. However, he did have a cave which he used to stable his animals, which was relatively clean--for a stable. They took it and asked Yahweh's blessing on the innkeeper.

A Premature Birth

Joseph learned where there was a midwife, Dinah bat Isaac. Joseph feared the worst. The birth was to be a month early. He ran for the midwife. As he ran, it seemed that everything else was suspended in time. The fowls in the air were suspended in flight; people seemed to be locked in suspended animation. Time seemed to stop. But Joseph found the midwife, who was able to get to the cave in time.

When the midwife arrived, Miriam's contractions were coming so close together that the child should be coming out. But Dinah found that the child was in the "feet-first position." One of the skills of the midwife was the ability to turn the child's body around in the mother's womb so that the birth could proceed naturally. Dinah was able to get the child turned around. Through it all, like a good Jewish mother, Miriam did not cry out at all. Finally, the baby came. It was a boy. Miriam thanked Yahweh that it was a boy. Boy babies were considered much more valuable than girl babies. Some day girls would leave home and therefore were considered a "false treasure." But Jews didn't kill girl babies the way many Gentiles did.

The child was delivered—premature and small, but healthy. Dinah cut the umbilical cord and gave the baby a spank on its bottom. It drew its first breath. Everyone broke into a relieved grin. There were tears of joy. Dinah washed the baby and rubbed it with oil and salt. Then the baby was officially presented to the father, who put the child on his knee, proudly affirming the boy's birthright. Dinah removed the amniotic sac and gave Miriam the usual saltwater douche, cleaned her up, and gave her the traditional postnatal refreshment of warm tea.

But after he was cleaned up, the baby let them know in no uncertain terms he was hungry. He was wrapped in the traditional way, in swaddling bands to keep his limbs straight. Miriam took him and nursed him—his first meal. As the midwife took the baby and put it in its unusual cradle, a feed trough, Miriam couldn't help but wonder what this child's future would be. Joseph was so excited, he could not think at all.

Having been told that the mother was still a virgin, the midwife met an elderly neighbor, Salome, and told her the story. Salome made fun of the story, but went to see the baby. For some unexplained reason, she was convinced. On the way home she had a mild stroke, paralyzing her right hand. Interpreting this as punishment for her doubts, she prayed to Yahweh to restore her and went back and held the child in her arms. The stroke abated. There was no rational explanation for her recovery.

Unlikely Witnesses

The next evening four shepherds arrived with a fantastic story about the appearance of angels, who informed them that they would find the "messiah" in a manger in Bethlehem. They honored the child and returned home. They enthusiastically told a number of people of their experience. Several people were amazed at what they heard, but ended up discussing the stories of other would-be messiahs, who were killed or who simply disappeared. After the initial euphoria, the shepherds were never heard of again, suggesting that they had had an ecstatic experience which burned out. However, Miriam could not get these things out of her mind. Surely her son was not the one to be the redeemer of Israel. On the other hand . . . .

CHAPTER 3

A CHAOTIC INFANCY

Circumcision and Cleansing

For a week family and friends celebrated in the traditional way. On the eighth day, the village *mohel,* a specialist in the process, circumcised the child. Becoming a Jew on the day of his circumcision, the boy received a name. Unlike the usual practice, they did not give him the name for his grandfather—or even his father. The child's birth was celebrated with the traditional ceremonies. On the eighth day of his life, Martius 29, the unnamed child was circumcised and named "Joshua." A second ceremony attended the birth. The mother was considered impure. Forty days later, she went to the temple to be purified and to sacrifice a lamb and a pigeon. Because her first-born son belongs to Yahweh, he had to be 'bought back' by paying the priest six silver shekels. Since it was a large sum to most, it was not unusual for priests to return it as a present. He graciously returned the money to Joseph.

Expanding the second temple into a magnificent building was one way Herod the Great's ways of attempting to elicit the devotion of the Jewish population. Ten thousand men had labored for years expanding the second temple. At the entrance was a sign warning Gentiles to go no farther on pain of death.

Inside was the women's court, which was as far as women and children could go. Inside that was the court of Israel, where only Jewish men could enter. The priest's court was the place where the altar was located, on which sacrifices were made. The inner part was divided into three chambers. The outside was the priestly court where sacrifices were made, what had been the outside court of the old Tabernacle. Past that was the holy place where incense was burned. Finally, the very inner-most part was the holy of holies, where the presence of Yahweh was supposed to dwell, and which was entered only once per year by the High Priest on the Day of Atonement.

In the original temple, the Holy of Holies was the place where the Ark of the Covenant had resided, containing the Ten Commandments, a jar of manna, and Aaron's rod. In 586 BCE, the Babylonians had destroyed Solomon's Temple. Nobody ever knew exactly what had happened to the Ark. *Second Maccabees* said that it was surreptitiously taken by priests and buried in a cave on Mt. Nebo. Another story is that it was taken by priests to Axum in Ethiopia.

Strange Predictions

Arriving at the Temple, Joseph and Miriam purchased a pair of doves and young pigeons as a sacrifice for the child's circumcision. His parents were startled when a man in the temple named Simeon proclaimed their child as the messiah. Simeon said that Yahweh had promised him that he would see the messiah before he died. He took the child in his arms and sang a song of thanksgiving:

"Sovereign Adonai, as you have promised
Now dismiss your servant in peace,
For my eyes have seen your salvation
Which you have prepared in the sight of
   all people,
A light for revelation to the Gentiles
And for glory to your people Israel."

But he also made a sorrowful prediction that the contention over the child would be the undoing of many in Israel and a sword would pierce his mother's soul. Joseph and Miriam were totally mystified by the words of Simeon. But that was not the last event to startle them on that day.

As they were leaving, they saw a woman named Anna bat Phanuel. She was a descendent of the tribe of Asher. She was eighty-four and had worshiped in the temple, fasting and praying, ever since her husband had died when she was twenty-three years old. Anna, too, pronounced a prayer of thanksgiving for the child and predicted that it would be the "redemption of Jerusalem." Joshua's parents were stunned by what they had heard from both Simeon and Anna. But these were not the first strange utterances they had heard about him.

Joseph's second cousin, Benjamin bar David, prevailed on him to move to Bethlehem. The carpenter had recently died and Bethlehem was desperate for someone to take his place. After agreeing, Joseph and Miriam returned to Nazareth to set things in order. After six months they moved their home and Joseph's tools to Bethlehem. By the time he returned, orders back-logged. For a while he had to work from daylight to dark to catch up.

But there was always time to stop for prayer three times a day, for reciting some of their favorite Psalms, for the Sabbath observance at the synagogue, and for rest on the Sabbath. By the time Joshua was a year old, he was walking and saying "Abba" (daddy) and "Aem" (mommy).

CHAPTER 4

HISTORY LEADING TO HEROD

Quirk of History
What quirk of history brought Herod to the throne when Joshua was born? It begins three centuries earlier. After the assassination of Philip of Macedonia in 336 BCE, his 22-year-old son, Alexander, invaded the Persian Empire. In 332 BCE, Alexander conquered Palestine. But after conquering all the way to India, Alexander died in June 323 BCE at age 32. His generals squabbled over division of the empire.
General Seleucus got Syria. Ptolemy got Egypt. In the wars between the Ptolemys and the Seleucids, Palestine was caught in the middle. But things turned really sour for the Jews when Antiochus IV Epiphanes seized the Seleucid throne.

A Madman Inspires Rebellion
In 167 BCE, Antiochus made the mistake of his life. He pushed Hellenization on the Jews, outlawing the Jewish religion. Although many Jews were enthralled with the Greek culture, they maintained their devotion to only one God, Yahweh. Antiochus ordered the worship of Zeus; profaned the temple by sacrificing a pig on the altar, dedicating it to Olympian Zeus; and would not allow Jews to keep the Sabbath or celebrate the traditional feasts. Copies of the Torah were burned. Women who circumcised their children were forced to walk through the city with their babies hanging around their necks and then they were thrown from the city wall. Some held Sabbath worship secretly in caves.
Syrian troops were sent into villages to enforce sacrifice to Zeus. In the village of Modein, a man named Mattathias killed the soldier in charge of enforcing Zeus worship and called for revo-

lution. His sons, Judas, Jonathan, and Simon Maccabeus led the revolt. They hid in the hills and carried out hit-and-run guerrilla warfare against the Seleucids. Judas captured Jerusalem, but was killed 160 BCE, and Jonathan took command of the revolt.

Jonathan Maccabeus supported the rebellion of Alexander Balas against the Seleucid ruler, Demetrius I, and was appointed the high priest. The high priest who was removed, Zadok ben Ami, withdrew a group of followers called Essenes, referring to himself as the Teacher of Righteousness. Jonathan was killed in 143 BCE and his brother, Simon, ruled until he was murdered by his son-in-law in 134 BCE. His son, John Hyrcanus became ruler and high priest (134-104 BCE).

Internal Political Strife

Many Jews did not accept Hyrcanus as king, because he was not descended from David. But in 128 BCE, he declared Jewish independence, attacked Shechem and Mount Gerizim, destroying the Samaritan Temple in 111 BCE, winning him the support of all but the most theological sticklers. He also carried on a military campaign against the Idumeans east of the Jordan River, forcing their conversions to Judaism. *This would have significant repercussions later.*

However, not all was rosy. The Pharisees opposed Hyrcanus' roles as high priest and ethnarch (political leader of the Jews). Pharisees were a religious-political party of mostly middle-class expert interpreters of the Torah. In addition to strict adherence to the Torah, they believed in angels, resurrection, and immortality of the soul. Hyrcanus was supported by the Sadducees, a religious-political party made up mostly of aristocratic priests. Later, Hyrcanus' eldest son, Aristobulus I, became high priest and the first Hasmonean to call himself "king." When Aristobulus died, his widow, Queen Salome Alexandra, married Alexander Jannaeus, Aristobulus' brother, whom he had previously imprisoned.

Jannaeus (ruled 103-76 BCE) was constantly involved in military conflict. He was opposed by the Pharisees for marrying his brother's widow. His soldiers killed more than six thousand rebels in the temple courtyard.

The Qumran community called for Jannaeus' overthrow, culminating in a Judean Civil War in 88 BCE, which lasted six years. Jannaeus cut the throats of the wives and children of eight hundred rebels in front of them and then crucified them as Jannaeus ate with his concubines.

A Woman Changes the Political Terrain

When Jannaeus died in 76 BCE, his wife, Salome Alexandra (139–67 BCE), ruled Judea in his place. She restored the Pharisees, who became Judea's ruling class, and appointed her eldest son, Hyrcanus II, high priest. Upon her death, Hyrcanus II succeeded to the throne. His younger brother, Aristobulus II, overthrew him and became high priest and king from 66 to 63 BCE.

An independent Jewish state ended, not because of invasion, but as a result of internecine strife between brothers. Both Hyrcanus and Aristobulus appealed to the Roman general Pompey, who conquered Jerusalem in 63 BCE and appointed Hyrcanus II "ethnarch" and later, high priest

But real political authority was in the hands of the Romans, represented by Antipater of Idumea. In 47 BCE, Herod, Antipater's son, went to Rome and obtained the support of Marc Antony and Octavian, who declared him king of Judea in 39 BCE.

A Foreigner on the Throne

Herod was born around 74 BCE, the second son of Antipater of Idumea, the desert kingdom just south of Judea. Ethnically, Idumeans were Edomites, descendents of Esau, but under John Hyrcanus (140–130 BCE) had adopted the Jewish religion. Herod was unpopular because he had supplanted the Hasmoneans, who despite their unpopularity, were true hereditary Jews. So, to gain favor with his subjects, he divorced his wife, Doris, and married a Hasmonean princess, Mariamne I.

Herod was still hated because of his brutality and decadence. He tried to gain acceptance by building a magnificent expansion of the temple, as well as an aqueduct to Jerusalem, fortresses at Masada and Herodium, and the city of Caesarea. He built *gymnasia* for Gentile cities, where boys were educated and where their athletic competition was in the nude, an offense to traditional Jews. He also built the Antonia fortress in Jerusalem quartering a few Roman troops and the palace where the Roman procurator stayed when he was in town.

Herod allowed the high priests to preside over the Great Sanhedrin, a council of seventy members whose decisions applied to Jews all over the world. It was comprised of members of the high priestly class, elders of the people, and scribes (doctors of the Torah) who decided civil, criminal, and religious issues.

But Herod was extremely paranoid and controlled his subjects by use of terror. In 29 BCE, he had his wife, Mariamne, and his brother-in-law, Kostobar, executed. In 7 BCE he had two of his sons, Aristobulus IV and Alexander, executed. In 4 BCE he executed Antipater III, his son by his first wife, Doris. Caesar Augustus once quipped that he would rather be Herod's pig than his son. When Herod died, the nation breathed a brief collective sigh of relief. However, after his death, riots erupted in Jerusalem, bringing Roman troops, who occupied Judaea and Samaria. Looking back, many wished for the "good old days" under Herod.

CHAPTER 5

UNLIKELY FOREIGN HONORS

Parthian Visitors

Joseph and Miriam were unaware of the fact that in Parthia, members of the Zoroastrian priestly class had been interpreting the position of the stars. They used the stars to foretell the future and to manipulate the fate of individuals and nations. Along with what they had heard from Jewish scholars in Persia (the location of the Parthian Empire), they interpreted the movement of the stars to point to the birth of a king in Judea. Five of them were sent by the king of Parthia to Judea to honor the new king and perhaps establish a treaty against Rome, Parthia's mortal enemy.

Baltasar, Caspar, Melchior, Aleister, and Abashar were the king's official representatives to the court of Judea. The group was relatively small in that each man took only two servants, and only four military escorts. They arrived in Judea's capital city, Jerusalem, when Joshua was about eighteen months old. Upon their arrival in Jerusalem, they established a temporary residence in a local inn. The next day, they visited King Herod.

Royal Paranoia and Intrigue

Because of his paranoia, when told of the Persian magis' mission, Herod assumed that there was a potential usurper in the land. But keeping his real feelings to himself, he called for his counselors to see if they knew anything about the birth of a king. The only specific prophecy they found was in the *Micah* scroll:

> "But you, Bethlehem, in the land of Judah,
> are by no means least among the rulers of Judah;
> for out of you will come a ruler
> who will be shepherd of my people Israel."

Although this was a slight misquote of the Hebrew scroll, it basically conveyed the idea. So, cunning paranoid that he was, Herod asked the magi to find the child and report back, so that he could honor him. Originally, the magi were fooled by Herod. They excitedly left for Bethlehem, arriving there early in the afternoon. If one wanted information, the bazaar was the place to go. It was not only the place of trade, but the place where scuttlebutt was easy to hear. Virtually everyone came to the market everyday to bargain for daily necessities. Elderly men came to hear the local gossip, drink tea, and socialize. It did not take the magi long to learn what births had occurred according to their astrological calculations.

The local Sanhedrin met briefly each day to address legal concerns. The inquiries of the magi gave them great concern. They begged the magi not to make trouble, fearing repercussions of a potential rival to Herod's throne, but would only hint at their fears. One did not make open, critical comments about Herod to people one was not sure could be trusted.

The magi perceived their fears from their cryptic remarks. Although they assured the Sanhedrin of Herod's good intentions, they knew enough about politicians to understand that one did not necessarily take what they said at face value. So when the magi arrived at Joseph's house, they were experiencing mixed emotions.

As Miriam served the magi on the roof, they explained to Joseph the purpose of their mission. Both Miriam and Joseph related the numerous strange incidents surrounding their son's birth. This clearly confirmed to the magi that this was the child for whom they were looking. Joseph and Miriam expressed their concern quite openly. They knew of the murders in Herod's family on the mere suspicion of sedition. Nevertheless, the magi presented to Joseph gifts for the child of gold, incense, and myrrh. Joseph reluctantly expressed his gratitude.

That night the magi's retinue camped outside the village. There was no inn in Bethlehem large enough to accommodate them. They discussed the issue of whether to return to Herod. Their concern was confirmed when Baltasar had a foreboding dream that night. The next morning, he shared the contents of the dream with the others. Along with all else they had heard, they interpreted it as a warning not to return to Herod.

Therefore, they surreptitiously used a route out of the country usually used only by the locals. It was rough terrain, but camels are sure-footed animals. They can reach a top speed for forty miles per hour, can run twenty-five miles per hour for an hour, and twelve miles per hour for eighteen hours. The magi left during late morning, urging their steeds at twenty-five mile per hour, making their way southeast toward Herodium.

In order to not arouse suspicion, they slowed their camels down when they saw someone ahead of them. Once they passed the traveler and were out of sight, they resumed their gallop. From Herodium they followed a wadi ten miles to the shores of the Lake Asphaltitis (Dead Sea), and from there to Engedi, where they stopped to eat a noon meal.

Early in the afternoon they made their way to Masada, fifteen miles south, where Herod had a detachment of soldiers stationed. It took them about an hour to get to Masada. They slowed down before they arrived at Masada, so that they would not attract unusual attention. The soldiers there knew nothing yet about the magi. Masada was a high fortress and as their camels ambled by Masada, they saw soldiers looking down at them. They gave a brief, friendly wave and received a wave in return.

In the next half hour, they had traveled another ten miles, crossed into the kingdom of Nabatea, now safe from Herod. By the evening, they were at the south end of Lake Asphaltitis, twelve hundred feet below sea level. The oppressive heat was trapped in the bowl made by that extension of the Great Rift Valley. In early evening the hot *sirocco* winds that funneled down the wadis from the east began to cool off. They decided to rest there.

That evening, moisture-laden clouds blew in from the Great Sea (Mediterranean) and clashed with the sirocco, creating a violent storm that dumped several inches of rain on the barren land, funneling large amounts of water down the wadis into Lake Asphaltitis. Not being acquainted with the local weather conditions, they had pitched their tents just above a rather shallow wadi. The water level rose so quickly, that they barely got their tents down and moved to higher ground. It was no fun having to make such maneuvers in a rain storm. But the situation was so critical that the magi had to help their servants get their tents pulled up and escape to higher ground. The deluge was short-lived. Once they got the tents up again, they fell on their wet rugs, exhausted, and slept late the next morning.

By the time they had breakfast, the wadis had already emptied and they could cross and continue their journey. They crossed the Zered River, a glorified wadi maintaining a trickle most of the year. The magi pushed their camels as fast as their advanced age would allow. It was twelve miles due east to the King's Highway. Once they got to that main thoroughfare, travel was much easier. It was fifteen miles to Kir-moab, another twenty to the ford in the Arnon River, six miles more north to Dibon, and twenty-five more to Hesh-bon, where they spent the night.

The next morning, they made it to Philadelphia, one of the Decapolis (Ten Cities), in two hours. There, they loaded supplies. Rather than continuing up to Damascus and taking the long way along the Fertile Crescent, they headed straight across the desert. It took four days to cross the Arabian Desert to Babylon on the Euphrates River. From there it was a short hop to their capital at Ctesiphon on the Tigris River.

They reported the results of their trip, which was a political disappointment to King Phraates. King Phraates IV ascended the Parthian throne in 37 BCE, after murdering his father and his thirty surviving brothers. When civil war erupted between Octavian and Antony, Phraates took Armenia, but lost it back when his own civil war broke out. He had hoped that, since Herod's friend, Mark Antony, had been killed by Octavian, Herod might be inclined to establish a treaty with Parthia against Caesar Augustus. But the magi determined that Herod was not a man to be trusted, so they returned without a treaty.

It is said that the magi took Jesus' swaddling clothes back home and sacrificed them to their god, Ahura Mazda, in the fires of the Zoroastrian religion, established by the Persian philosopher, Zarathustra. The tradition also says that the clothes did not burn up, so they used them as a religious artifact. However, by then Joshua was no longer wearing swaddling clothes. The story, while charming, is no more than pious legend.

The Great Escape

Joseph, too, had had a sleepless night, drifting in and out of foreboding dreams. In a dream he saw an angel who urged him to escape to Egypt. He awoke with a start, not knowing whether the dream was a legitimate portent or not. But he knew enough about Herod to err on the side of caution. Early on the morning of September (Cheshvan) 28, 5 BCE, Joseph quickly packed personal necessities, a few tools, and borrowed a donkey from Benjamin. He had built a crib to fit on the back of a donkey. Two donkeys would carry their belongings and one would carry the sleeping child.

"Miriam! Get up. We have to leave."

Groggily, she asked, "Why? What is wrong?"

"I had a dream that it is too dangerous here for the child," Joseph warned.

"What? Are you crazy?" She was no longer groggy, but fully awake.

For five minutes they talked about what Herod might do and the role that dreams had played in their lives. They concluded that caution was the better part of valor: They would leave. Miriam helped Joseph finish packing and put the child in the donkey crib. The parents would walk. The child would ride. As the donkey began to bump along, Joshua awoke and began to cry. Miriam took him and walked a few minutes, patting him on the back, and softly singing a psalm. Joshua fell asleep and was returned to his crib, where he slept for the rest of the night.

Fortunately, there was a full moon. They took that as a sign that Yahweh was with them. It was an uphill fifteen miles to Hebron, but they were in a hurry and made it by sun-up. When they arrived, they immediately headed for the square, where they could refresh themselves at the well; and where townsfolk could invite travelers to their homes. Abraham bar Nun invited them into his home. Joseph and Miriam sensed immediately that they could share their predicament with him and his family. They were right.

"Take some food. Refresh yourselves," Abraham insisted. "Get a good night's sleep and get up early tomorrow morning. It will still be cool. If you are not in Gaza by noon, rest during the heat of the day. Sarah! Bring them water to wash their feet and bring oil for their heads."

Abraham's older daughters were already bringing goats' milk, bread, and honey. Their hunger and exhaustion made the food taste particularly delicious. They slept for about four hours and continued their journey, being sent off with prayers of Adonai's blessing. The next part of the journey was less arduous. It was thirty-five miles from Hebron to Gaza, down-hill all the way. That made the walking easier, but as they descended, it became hotter.

The Deceiver is Deceived

Herod had been anxious for the return of the magi. He assumed that they had spent the night and would return the next day. But by noon, he dispatched a *contubernium* of soldiers to Bethlehem. A contubernium was the smallest group in the army, who shared a tent. When they arrived, they learned that the magi had visited Miriam and Joseph. The decanus, Julius, leader of eight, led the men into the house. The evidence was clear. The magi had deceived Herod. It seemed obvious that Joseph and Miriam had made a hasty evacuation. The *decanus* quickly found Joseph's relatives.

"Where is the man Joseph?" the decanus asked Benjamin.

"Are they not at home? I think they were going to Jerusalem," Benjamin lied nonchalantly and was very convincing.

The fact that the Parthian magi had visited Joseph and Miriam, and that neither they nor the magi could be found, was circumstantial evidence--but not conclusive. The decanus sent a rider back to Herod. Upon arriving in Jerusalem, the rider immediately reported to Herod. Herod went into a rage and ordered that two other contubernium be sent to Bethlehem to kill all boys less than two years of age. The next morning they arrived in Bethlehem and rounded up all the boys. Twelve male babies and toddlers were executed to satisfy Herod's maniacal paranoia. Joseph's nephew, Jonathan, was one of the casualties.

Exodus to Egypt

Meanwhile, Joseph and Miriam arrived in Gaza after two days and nights on the road. Gaza was in the Roman province controlled by Egypt, a bustling village on the main trade route between Mesopotamia and Egypt.

In Gaza they boarded a small actuaria, a fast cargo ship carrying olive oil, figs, and wine to Tanis, Egypt. The actuaria was so fast because it used both a square sail and oars. The hundred-fifty miles from Gaza to Tanis took a day-and-a-half. It was a pleasant trip because the exhausted parents were able to rest. They wanted to sleep, but little Joshua was fascinated by the swan head that decorated the curved stern. He kept saying, "Look mommy. Look mommy." Finally, he too became too tired to stay awake. In their exhaustion, the three of them slept for almost an entire day.

When they awoke, Joseph and Miriam both felt refreshed and safe. Before long, they arrived at Tanis. It was afternoon. They found an inn for the night. Another peaceful night. They sang a psalm of thanksgiving before drifting off. Yahweh had protected them again. Miriam tried to think about all that she had heard about her son, but her body would not allow it. Exhausted, she drifted off and . . . .

CHAPTER 6

A NEW LIFE

Life in Tanis

Joseph woke up early, just before daybreak. He looked out the window through the foggy haze at the series of splintering channels of the Nile Delta that leads to the Great Sea, what the Romans called *Mare Nostrum*, "Our Sea." Joseph thought about that name and chuckled at the arrogance. But right now he felt safe in the *Pax Romana,* "Roman Peace." For most, *Pax Romana* was an illusion. It applied only to Roman citizens. Others within the realm of the Roman Empire were subject to the whim of the authorities. Conquered people were subject to the whim of the Roman soldiers, who could rape and bully at their pleasure. There was no recourse in the courts. Only Roman citizens were guaranteed civil rights. But for Joseph and Miriam, any other place in the Roman Empire was safer than in Judea, ruled by the paranoid monster.

"But," Joseph wondered, "what lies ahead of us in Tanis?"

For Jews, Tanis had an interesting history. The patriarch, Jacob, brought his family to Egypt sometime before 1700 BCE, during the rule of the foreign Hyksos, and settled in the Nile Delta an area they called the "Land of Goshen." In about 1570 BCE, the Hyksos were driven out and an ethnic Egyptian dynasty returned to the throne in Lower Egypt, the area closest to the Great Sea. During the early Nineteenth Egyptian Dynasty, probably during the rule of Seti I (1302-1290 BCE), Israelite refugees escaped from Egypt under the leadership of Moses in what is commonly known as the Exodus.

Tanis was located in the northeastern part of the Nile Delta. During the time that Joseph and Miriam lived in Tanis, it was an important commercial center. Joseph woke Miriam. "I'm going to find the market and buy some food. We particularly need milk for Joshua."

"Good. We do not have enough food to last us today," Miriam responded drowsily.

The innkeeper, Neco Alexander, had just gotten up and was helpful in directing Joseph to the market. Since he had no job, Joseph was sparing in how much he spent. Because of the haste of their escape, they had had to leave a lot of their belongings in Bethlehem. Unlike day laborers, Joseph was able to save a few shekels from his carpentry. The gold given Joshua by the magi would ordinarily be enough to keep them for a half year. But there were a number of essentials to be bought, including some of the larger tools that Joseph was not able to load onto the donkey. He whispered a prayer of thanks to Yahweh for His providence.

At the market, Joseph purchased bread, cheese, milk, some dates, three figs, and olive oil. As he bartered with the merchants, he made inquiries about work, learning that there were at least two carpenters who may need help. One was a Jew, Solomon bar Penuel. The other was an Egyptian named Farik. Joseph felt more comfortable working with a member of his faith, so he decided to visit Solomon after he broke the fast.

Miriam was overjoyed to see the figs. Considering their situation, she did not expect even this slight delicacy. They prayed for Yahweh's blessing on their meal. Miriam gave a small cup of milk and small portions of cheese, bread, and olive oil to Joshua. She and Joseph chuckled as Joshua got the oil all over his hands and decorated his face around his mouth with it. Miriam wiped his hands and mouth. Joshua loved figs. He pointed saying, "Want fig."

"Finish your cheese and bread first. And drink your milk. Then you can have your fig." A typical mother!

Joshua grabbed the cup of goat's milk, spilled a little and gulped it, some running down his chin on to his chest. Another couple of chuckles and another wipe.

"Slow down, Joshua. The fig will wait," assured Joseph.

"Well," chided Miriam good-naturedly, "he's just like his father."

"Hmmmm," grunted Joseph. He had no retort. Changing the subject, he continued, "I learned about two carpenters who might need an assistant."

"Oh! Wonderful," exclaimed Miriam. "So soon."

"Well, let's not count our pigs before they squeal." It was a particularly Jewish figure of speech . . . just a little naughty. They would never say it in front of a rabbi.

"Fig," Joshua repeated. He was finished with the bread, cheese, and milk, some of which actually got into his mouth.

"Here," offered Miriam.

Joshua grabbed it and tore into it ravenously.

"Slow down, Joshua. Don't eat like a Samaritan," chided Joseph.

Joshua wondered what that meant.

"Joseph, don't say such things in front of the boy. He could develop a bad attitude toward Samaritans. Not all Samaritans are bad people. Many are just like you and me. They are Adonai's children too."

Joshua wondered what that meant. His education was beginning. He would never remember the specific statement, but it was now planted somewhere in his brain.

Beginning a New Life

The sun was beginning to heat up and the smell of dead fish began to waft over the inn. They had brought the aromatic myrrh and frankincense presented to Joshua by the magi. They came in handy to cover the dead fish odor in the air.

"I had better try to find Solomon," said Joseph. "From the directions I got, his shop should not be hard to find."

"Adonai grant you success, honey," encouraged Miriam.

"Bye, daddy."

"Bye, Joshua." He hugged his wife and son and left.

Joseph was right. He easily found Solomon's carpentry shop. The shop was just below Solomon's living area. He was not encouraging. "I would be glad to give you a few part-time projects, but I do not need full-time help. If I can give you a little work to get you by, I will be glad to do it."

Joseph thanked him for the offer and assured him that if he could not get full-time employment, he would be thankful for any work that Solomon would give him. He headed off for Farik's shop. It was not in the part of the city where the Jews lived, but he found Farik without any trouble. Farik was a jolly man of about 45 or 50. What little gray hair was left circled his head, leaving a bald dome on top. Farik spoke Egyptian with his family and friends. There was evidence everywhere of his devotion to the Egyptian goddess Isis. But he was completely Hellenized culturally. Like most Egyptians he spoke good Egyptian Koine (Common) Greek.

The Hellenization of Egypt

As Alexander the Great's juggernaut had rolled across the eastern Mediterranean and beyond, he left the mark of Hellenism wherever he went. In 332 BCE he was received in Egypt as a liberator and god. Not all Persians were like Cyrus the Great, who was very tolerant of other peoples' religion. He had even financed the return of Jews to Jerusalem in 516 BCE and paid for the repair of the Jewish temple. But after Cyrus things were different. For two centuries the Egyptians had suffered oppression by the Persians, who tore down their temples, ridiculed their gods, and instituted a heavy tax burden.

Alexander, on the other hand, offered a sacrifice to Apis, their sacred bull. He initiated a separation of power between the civilian and military government in such a way that it prevented corruption. Even peasants could appeal directly to the king if money was extorted from them. Egyptian officials were allowed to freely administer Egyptian affairs, under the supervision of Macedonians.

As long as they did an adequate job, Egyptian officials had a free hand to run the government. Alexander was crowned as pharaoh in Siwa, three hundred miles west of the place where the Nile River breaks into a delta. He established a new town on the western Nile Delta, to be a center of trade between Egypt, Arabia, and India in the east and the western Mediterranean. The magnificent port, which he modestly named Alexandria, was to become a center of culture and learning. He established one of the world's great libraries of the time and on Pharos, the island that protected the harbor of Alexandria, a great lighthouse was built that was considered by the great Greek historian, Herodotus, to be one of the seven wonders of the ancient world. The Egyptians couldn't have been more pleased. Probably nowhere in Alexander's conquering expeditions did Hellenism take root like it did in Egypt. Therefore, only the most isolated people in Egypt were unable to speak some Greek.

On June 13, 323 BCE, on his deathbed Alexander was asked who should be his successor. "To the most worthy," was his answer. Not very helpful. Rejecting several possible successors within Alexander's family, his principal generals divided the empire among themselves. Syria (including Judea) went to Seleucus, and Ptolemy got Egypt. Egypt prospered under his long reign. However, the generals who had gotten along so well under Alexander descended into warfare.

Ptolemy established an Alexandrian museum and a university, at which none other than Euclid and Archimedes taught. Alexandria was a major center of trade from Ethiopia and deep in Africa; Arabia, Mesopotamia, and India; and the western Mediterranean. Ptolemy introduced Greek banking methods and the use of silver coins. He respected the Egyptians' religion also. Although the poor did not benefit appreciably from the burgeoning economy, because Ptolemy and his successors did not oppress them, they too were relatively satisfied.

Because Herod's domain had also been Hellenized, Joseph learned to speak Koine Greek reasonably well. In his business, Joseph came into contact with numerous ethnic peoples, all of whom spoke some Greek. He even learned a few Latin phrases but could not really communicate in Latin.

Joshua's Egyptian Education

When Joseph went to interview with Farik regarding a job, the two men liked each other immediately. Joseph had a job. It would not be close to home, but he would enjoy working with Farik. But on Aprilis 10, 5 BCE (Nissan), not long after he began working with Farik, Joseph's options changed. Word came that Herod had died on Aprilis 1.

Joseph's second cousin, Benjamin, wrote informing him that Herod Archelaus had become ethnarch of Judea, Samaria, and Idumea. He was brutal like his father. Protests resulted in his troops killing 3000 rioters. Varus, the Roman prefect, controlled the unrest in Jerusalem. Archelaus sought and crucified 2000 more of them. So Joseph's cousin, Benjamin, did not recommend that Joseph return to Bethlehem.

The prefect ruled from Caesarea, but established a small Roman garrison at the Antonia Fortress in Jerusalem, overlooking the temple court. Judaea was directly ruled by the Sanhedrin. During the major festivals, the Roman prefect brought additional troops to Jerusalem. At festivals, the possibility of insurrection was particularly acute. Major seditious acts occurred at the Feast of Weeks in 40 BCE, and again at the Passover and the Feast of Weeks in 4 BCE (only a few months after Joshua was born). When riots did occur, the legate sent an additional four legions (about 20,000 infantry and 5,000 cavalry) to Jerusalem.

Not long after he heard from Benjamin, Joseph received a letter from his brother, Ishmael, that Herod Antipas (another son of Herod the Great), who had become tetrarch* of Galilee, was less

---

* "Originally meant 'ruler of a fourth' or 'one of four rulers.' Used loosely for petty rulers, lower than 'ethnarch.' – Francisco O. Garcia-Treto. Bible Dictionary (Paul J. Achtemeier, Ed.), p. 1112."

despotic than his father and brother. Antipas was married to the daughter of Aretas, the powerful king of Nabatea, a kingdom south and east of Lake Asphaltitis (the Dead Sea). Ishmael encouraged Joseph to return to Nazareth. But for the time being, Joseph was not ready to travel again. He wanted some semblance of stability for a while.

A New Baby in the Family

They had been in Tanis for less than a year, in 2 BCE, when Miriam had another baby, named Jacob ("James" in Greek). The three-year-old Joshua was delighted to have a little brother. By the time he was four, he was trying to carry the ten-month-old Jacob. It looked very uncomfortable to the parents, seeing Joshua holding Jacob under his arms with Jacob's feet dangling near the ground. But Jacob did not seem to mind. Joshua was making a transition from the being cared for to caring for someone else. As he grew, he enjoyed becoming a mentor for his little brother.

Joshua Learned Medicine

Joshua began to learn about medicine at a very young age. He learned from the Egyptians, Greeks, and the Israelites. For most ancient cultures, disease was considered to be caused by hostile magic or the violation of a taboo. Among the Israelites, it was more apt to be considered punishment by Yahweh for some offence. In virtually all cultures, medicine was in the hands of the priesthood. In *The Surgical Papyrus*, a document developed sometime between 1720-1550 BCE in Egypt, some real elements of empirical medicine were recorded. In addition to that, the Egyptians had learned from the teaching of the great Greek physician Hippocrates.

Hippocrates was born into a family of doctors on the island of Cos in about 460 BCE. He established a medical school, covering topics on illnesses, treating patients with both diet and drugs, surgical methods, and medical ethics. He used science in medical care rather than superstition. As a result of the invasion of Alexander the Great, Hippocrates' teachings on medicine were introduced in

Egypt. The library in Alexandria had all the volumes produced by Hippocrates and many aspiring doctors went there to study.

Certain herbs, capers, mandrakes, castor oil, and garlic were some of the earliest "medicines." While Joshua was in Egypt, he had an Egyptian friend named Farouk, whose father was a priest-physician. Any time Joshua was not with Joseph in his carpenter's shop, he and Farouk spent time with Farouk's father. Since he was teaching Farouk to be a physician, by listening to Farouk's father, Joshua was able to learn much about Egyptian and Greek healing. He lived in the Land of Goshen, where a major disease was schistosomiasis, carried by a river fluke in the Nile Delta, was rampant. Egyptian physicians were able to heal people afflicted with it. As Joshua grew and read the *Exodus* and *Leviticus* scrolls, he learned about Israelite healing also.

The belief that disease was punishment by Yahweh meant that when one recovered, it was a sign that Yahweh was reconciled to the person. This belief hampered Israelite priests from trying to learn effective ways to use healing herbs. On the other hand, the faith in Yahweh's ability to heal clearly illustrated the ability of the psyche to affect one's physical condition positively.

For example, eight centuries earlier, Isaiah had told King Hezekiah that Yahweh said he was about to die. According to the story, Hezekiah wept and prayed, reminding Yahweh that he had been a faithful servant. So Yahweh changed his mind and Hezekiah lived another fifteen years.

Purity was also an important aspect of Israelite medical treatment. One could only remove uncleanness through purification by water. Such a practice obviously contributed to the health of the Israelites. And their hyper use of quarantine made them safe from communicable diseases. "Leprosy" (Hebrew: *tsaarath*) was a condition that required quarantine until the priest determined that the person was healed. The term described several conditions including fungus, ringworm, and psoriasis. Generally, uncleanness was not a sanitation issue, but a taboo. Nevertheless, leprosy did inspire fear of contagion. The touching of blood was considered to make one unclean. That taboo prevented Israel from developing the use of surgery.

A "withered hand" described maladies like strokes or polio. There were also instances of psychological problems, like hysterical paralysis. It seems that bubonic plague may have struck the Philistines during the time of Eli and Samuel eleven centuries earlier. When the Philistines returned the Ark of the Covenant to Israel, they gave an offering of gold tumors and five gold mice. The plague was carried along trade routes by rats, especially on shipments of food.

The Bubonic plague may also have been the disease that mysteriously wiped out the Assyrian army and caused them to withdraw from Jerusalem when they had it and King Hezekiah surrounded, as Sennacherib put it, "like a bird in a cage."

The procedure for dealing with impurity was fairly simple. The priest examined the disease, prescribed the treatment (which often involved quarantine), and assessed an offering, the fee for services. There were also numerous prohibitions about eating certain animals based on whether they had cloven hooves and chewed their cud, regulations which had no rational basis. Even the prohibition against eating pork was more a taboo against Canaanite practices than avoiding trichinosis.

In addition to providing light for homes, cooking, preserving leather, and anointing the heads, olive oil was used in medical care. It protected the skin from the sun and healed burns, wounds, and abrasions. Animal fat, copper acetate, wine, and honey were also used in treating bacterial infections. Alum in ground-powder form was used to protect the eyes from bacteria carried by flies and other insects. Frankincense and myrrh both burn, giving off a pleasant aroma. But they were also used to heal wounds.

Joshua also knew there was a great psychological power in faith to heal physical as well as psychological maladies, both of which were thought to be the influence of evil spirits.

Joshua Loved Egypt

Joshua loved the Nile Delta. It was full of life. It is a rich agricultural region, intensively farmed for at least three thousand years. But that didn't concern Joshua in the least. He loved the Egyptian lotus when they matured. He enjoyed chasing little gulls and whiskered terns when they migrated there during the winter. He particularly liked chasing grey herons, egrets and ibises, because they looked so funny when they ran. He could never catch them. They always headed for the water to escape. He didn't want to hurt them, just chase them. Turtles were easy to catch and play with, but he almost never caught frogs. They were too quick for him. When he did catch one, it always squirmed and kicked until it got away.

He loved to watch the hippopotami. When they were in the water and blew water out of their noses, it sprayed like a fountain. It made him giggle. He knew that "hippopotamus" meant "river horse." He thought it would be funny to see them race in a hippodrome. He chuckled to himself as he imagined himself riding a hippo in a hippodrome race. But there was one animal that was not so funny. His parents told him that when he saw a crocodile, he should run away as fast as he could. Although Joshua's parents warned him to be careful of crocodiles, one couldn't be totally vigilant all the time—especially a young, adventuresome boy. One day Joshua and his friend, Farouk, were fishing a mile or so from where they lived. It was a good day for fishing.

"I like the marshy Delta, don't you, Joshua?" quizzed Farouk.

"Yeah. I love to fish." Joshua turned toward Farouk and grinned one of those far-away grins that betrayed something near ecstasy.

"Were there rivers to fish in where you lived before?" Farouk asked.

"I don't remember," Joshua answered. "I was too young to remember."

"Don't you remember anything about Bethlehem?" Farouk asked, amazed.

"No. Not much. I just seem to remember what some places and people looked like. But I'm not sure." He hesitated. "Be quiet! You're scaring the fish."

"I'm not scaring fish. I've caught more fish than you," Farouk exulted.

Joshua rolled his eyes back. "Big deal! That won't last long," Joshua assured him. "Besides, I caught the two biggest ones."

"That won't last long either," retorted Farouk.

Turtles were easy to catch and play with, but he almost never caught frogs. They were too quick for him. When he did catch one, it always squirmed and kicked until it got away.

The boyhood banter of the two six-year-olds continued virtually unabated for over an hour, only interrupted periodically by the catch of another fish. In fact, they were so focused on what they were doing that they didn't notice two eyes seemingly floating just above water. A mid-sized crocodile slithered effortlessly through the water, barely causing a ripple.

"I got another one!" Farouk bellowed with delight. "It's a big one. I can tell. It's pulling really hard."

Joshua focused on the splashing. The fish came bursting up out of the water, tail grasping for water to propel it, coming down with a gigantic splash. It almost pulled Farouk in.
"It is a big one," Joshua thought. "It's bigger than mine. Farouk will never stop bragging." Then his thoughts were again directed toward the excitement of the scuffle.
The fish was about to pull Farouk in. "I need help," he pleaded. Joshua grabbed the line. They both pulled with all their might. As they got the fish near the bank, the line snapped as the fish disappeared into a great, gaping cavern. The broken line caused them to go sprawling backward. It was a crocodile. The fish was gone. The croc focused on the boys. They looked like a much more filling meal than the fish. Both boys got up stumbling over each other. Joshua recovered quickly and began to run. The crocodile was chasing a limping Farouk. He had sprained his ankle. The crocodile was gaining on him. Joshua turned back and began to yell at the top of his voice. It distracted the crocodile. It started toward Joshua, remembered Farouk, and began to return toward its original prey. Jesus screamed even louder, waiving his hands in the air. The croc paused. He seemed to be trying to determine which would be the more appetizing lunch. Joshua's racket helped make its decision. As Farouk escaped, the crocodile chased Joshua, who scrambled up a small cypress tree. The crocodile, with great patience, circled back and forth around the tree for what seemed to Joshua to be hours.
But within twenty minutes, Joseph came running with two of the pharaoh's soldiers. The soldiers, experienced in croc-fighting, knew just what to do. As the crocodile made its way toward one soldier, he threw his spear with unerring accuracy, piercing deep into the crocodile's open throat. The second soldier threw his spear with precision into the softer armor of the croc's side. The crocodile thrashed in a frenzy for a while, until the spear in its throat strangled it. It finally lay under the tree, inert, eyes open, still staring as if it was still on the prowl for young boys.

Joseph reached up to meet Joshua's out-stretched hands. They boy nestled in Joseph's arms wrapping his legs around his father's waist for all he was worth. He was crying uncontrollably. Joseph was unable to choke back his own tears. Miriam finally caught up. She was frantic. The dead crocodile, along with Farouk's frantic tale, made Miriam's heart pound uncontrollably with terror. She reached for Joshua and Joseph reluctantly surrendered him to his mother.

"This is the last time you go fishing without your father," her voiced trembled. A typical mother!

"Now Miriam, I am afraid for him too. But the boy has to learn to be vigilant. You can't keep him tied to your skirt forever," Joseph rejoined with authority. A typical father! And the father was the final authority in raising a son.

"You will be more careful next time, wont you Joshua?" he asked rhetorically.

Joshua was regaining his composure. His father trusted him. He grinned from ear to ear. "Yes, father," he assured. As he slowly shook his head back and forth, he said, "I will always be watching for crocodiles. I don't think I could ever forget that they are around."

Yes! There were dangers in Egypt, but Joshua loved his life in Egypt.

CHAPTER 7

CHILD GROWS IN WISDOM AND STATURE

The Toddler's Education Begins

Joshua continued to grow in wisdom and stature and in favor with Yahweh and man. Much of that growth in wisdom had to do with the nurturing he was given by his parents.

By the time Joshua was three years old, he had learned to sing a number of psalms. His parents told him the stories of Adam and Eve, of Abraham, Isaac, Jacob, Joseph, Moses, David, the Maccabees, and the prophets. They reminded him often that Yahweh stands with the poor and the powerless. They pointed out that they were poor but that there were many people who were much poorer than they were. They told him that the rich have laws passed to benefit them and that the poor are at their mercy. They told him how the prophets Amos, Isaiah, Malachi, Micah, Zephaniah, Zechariah, and Hosea condemned people who took advantage of the poor or turned their backs on the plight of the poor. This made an impression on Joshua. By the time he was three, he could quote the Commandments, but did not understand many of them. On the other hand, the commandments to love Yahweh with all your heart, soul, and mind and to love your neighbor as yourself, was in a general way, very clear. Over the years he would come to understand the two great commandments in more specific ways.

His parents were particularly good in understanding child development. During the first few months of the child's life, he was, like every other child, completely egocentric, the center of his world. He communicated his fears, his pain, and his hunger by crying. Both Miriam and Joseph understood that they should be attentive parents. By three weeks he was smiling back at them. By four weeks, Joshua was babbling. They smiled and talked to him a lot. The parents, especially his mother, held him when he cried.

They repeated "aem" ("mommy") and "abba" ("daddy") to him often. By the end of third month, he was trying to respond to their talking to him. By age one, he began to associate the words with the persons. Miriam and Joseph talked to the toddler a great deal. His parents demonstrated and explained many things, such as how to eat and how to catch a ball rolled to him. He began to develop a capacity for receptive language. At one year, he had a vocabulary of nineteen words; at two years, about three hundred words. He could form two-word sentences. "Daddy bye-bye?" he would ask. And he could put subject and object in correct order – "See camel." By the time he was three years old, Joshua had a vocabulary of well over a thousand words and at four he had spoke over sixteen hundred words.

Like most babies, at nine months he experienced anxiety regarding adults that were not familiar to him, but by fifteen months, he was over his fear. At fifteen months, he was walking steadily. The problem is, with his new-found freedom, he could get into things he shouldn't. Miriam and Joseph had to be very careful what they left lying around. His insatiable curiosity led to trouble at times, for which they mildly scolded him. He had to learn two things--that some things are not appropriate and that his will was subordinate to the wishes of his parents. Learning these little facts can save a child's life.

The Nile Delta was a snake-infested area. One day, as Miriam was preparing the evening meal, Joshua was playing, banging two bronze plates together. Then he noticed an object that had entered the room. He got up and began to walk toward it. Relieved that the racket had stopped, Miriam turned to see what Joshua was doing. There she saw an Egyptian cobra reared up in front of Joshua. Joshua was reaching for it. Miriam screamed the only thing she could think to say.

"No!" she screamed.

The scream startled both the snake and Joshua, who began to cry. Miriam threw a clay pot at the cobra. The loud sound of breaking pottery and the feeling of broken shards hitting its body disoriented the serpent. It half-turned to attack the pottery. Miriam grabbed the crying child to get him out of the way. She then got a hoe and killed the snake.

She took the crying toddler in her arms and said, "Bad snake. Bad snake."

By the time Joseph got home, Joshua was not longer crying, but Miriam was. She explained the reason for her tears. The two of them thanked Yahweh for saving their child. They rehearsed some "what ifs." If Joshua hadn't been banging pots and quit, she wouldn't have bothered to turn and look. If she had just frozen upon seeing the snake. If she had no pot available. If the snake had ignored the pot. If . . . . No! Yahweh had been protecting him.

There she saw an Egyptian cobra reared up in front of Joshua. Joshua was reaching for it. Miriam screamed the only thing she could think to say. "No!"

Two months later, Joshua was playing outside. He came running into the house in the stiff-legged way that toddlers do, hollering at the top of his lungs, "Mommy! Bad snake! Bad snake!"

Miriam and Joseph raced to the door, to see another cobra. Joseph quickly grabbed a hoe and killed it. The parents were so relieved to see that their son was remembering experiences and applying them to new situations, especially when issues of danger were involved And although he had developed trust, it was not uncritical trust.

Their interest in the things he did made him feel that what he was doing was important. He became as delighted as they were to see his accomplishments. Over time, Joshua learned to look at the world in a realistic way. As he did, they expressed their pleasure at his accomplishments.

By the time he was four, he could ask questions very clearly in full sentences. He loved the stories of the Adam and Eve, Abraham, and Israel's history. He particularly liked the story of how Moses was hidden in the bulrushes and how his big sister looked after him. He thought the story about Yahweh giving the Ten Commandments on the mountain and the story about the Golden Calf were exciting. He also liked the stories about Joshua's conquests, a man who had the same name as his.

Joshua particularly liked the story of how Moses was hidden in the bulrushes and how his big sister looked after him.

Parental Influence on Joshua

As he grew, his parents set examples of integrity, honesty, care for other people, especially the poor, and devotion to Yahweh. As time went on, he internalized their values. They were authoritative parents, who explained their reasoning and inspired confidence, rather than authoritarian parents whose demands are arbitrary and who wield brute power. So Joshua complied out of the desire to receive their approval rather than out of fear. By the time he was four, he began to notice something else about his parents.

Often, when they had very pleasurable food, Joshua would scarf his down. When he expressed his disappointment at the fact that his food was gone, they would often give him some of theirs. He gladly took it. But he thought that his parents were the dumbest people in the world for giving up something that tasted so good. However, by the time he was eight, he began to realize that they did it because of their love for him. They were willing to give up something pleasurable in order to give him pleasure. When he came to that insight, he was astounded that anyone could love that much. He couldn't imagine being like that, but he hoped some day he would be.

Wherever Joseph was, Joshua was with him. At three years old, he showed interest in what his father was doing. Joseph would drive a peg in slightly, and let Joshua drive it further. He used two hands and missed the peg often. Later, when they moved to Nazareth, Joseph went to the iron-smith in Sepphoris and had him make a small hammer-head for Joshua.

After the ironsmith had made the hammerhead, Joseph attached it to a handle. Now while Joseph was working, Joshua could bang away to his heart's content—first with both hands, later with one. With repetition, he got much better. Joseph noticed that Joshua was left-handed, a good omen. It was also considered an advantage in battle.

"Practice doesn't make *perfect,* but it does make *better.* And you are getting much better," Joseph would assure him.

He also let Joshua use his small saw and plane and other tools. He always explained how to use them safely. But even at that, some cuts, abrasions, and bruises were inevitable.

Joshua delighted in his "work"—except when he hit his thumb. Joseph would stop in the middle of any activity to comfort Joshua. Then he would send Joshua to Miriam, who would provide further comfort. After a time of wound-licking, he would be right back out in the shop under foot. Joseph was rarely cross at the inconveniences that Joshua created at times. He took great pride in his son's interest in "the old man's business."

Joshua also had to learn to play with other children. When he was still very young, like other children, he took toys away from others. When he did that, his parents would take the toy away from him and give it back to the other child and say, "Oh, Joshua. We don't take things away from people."

He would "throw a fit," but it did him no good. Over time, he learned the rules, and even came to agree with them and the values behind them.

But life would change. One day, when Joshua was about six (1 CE), his father and mother said they had something important to talk about with him.

"Joshua," his father said very seriously. "I want to talk to you about an important decision that your mother and I have made. For several years, your Uncle Ishmael has encouraged us to return to our original home in Nazareth. I know you will miss your friends, but you will have cousins there. And it is our home. We like it here in Tanis, but it is not home. We miss our home. We are moving to Nazareth."

Joshua did not want to go, but the decision had been made. He told his friends good-bye. A few days later they left for Nazareth.

CHAPTER 8

THE RETURN

The Trip Back Home

After five years in Egypt, in 3 CE, Joseph and Miriam returned to Nazareth. It was a much easier and quicker journey by boat than over land. But it was not short. So the day after the Sabbath, they boarded a river liburnian. It was lighter than most sea-going vessels and could maneuver in the shallow waters of the Nile Delta. This one was a Roman military patrol boat that carried dispatches up and down river. They had to take the liburnian about one hundred fifty miles west along the mouth of the delta to Alexandria. It took about four days from Tanis in the Delta to the Great Sea and west to Alexandria.

From Alexandria they took a hexerene, the main Roman military fleet flagship. It was the largest ship class in the Roman navy. The one they took was the admiral's personal flagship. Hexerenes usually had a contingent of sixty marines, but could handle one hundred fifty in emergencies. It had about six rows of rowers of fifty to one hundred rowers each.

But this particular hexerene was not heading for battle. It was going to Caesarea on a routine mission, transporting a contingent of Roman soldiers and had just a few marines. Civilians were sometimes boarded on military ships when they were not on a strictly military assignment. It was a way for a sea captain to make a little extra money. The trip was about six hundred miles directly across the eastern Mediterranean to Caesarea and took five days.

Joshua thoroughly enjoyed the trip. One of the Roman soldiers, Quintus Meridius, took particular interest in him, talking to Joshua about some of his experiences. Since the eastern Mediterranean had been relatively peaceful, there were no major battles he could brag about. But he showed Joshua the ship.

"Jesus, would you like to see the rowers below deck?" asked Quintus.

Joshua understood that his name in Greek was "Jesus."

"Yes," he said excitedly.

Quintus took him below to see the rowers. It was not what Joshua expected. The Roman fleet rowers were ordinarily of free status. Galley slaves were usually not at the oars, except when there were serious manpower problems. But these particular slaves were Parthian mariners who had been captured in the Persian Gulf. There were rows of men chained together. Their blank eyes looked exhausted and hopeless. He had seen a few slaves before, but they had been in Jewish and Roman homes and seemed to be well cared for. But these people looked like they were suffering inhuman treatment. Quintus continued to explain in glowing terms things of which Joshua believed he should be ashamed.

Like the rest of the soldiers, Quintus had very few duties on board ship, so he was able to give considerable attention to Joshua. He showed Joshua the marines' quarters, the admiral's quarters, and where the food was prepared. Joshua was interested, but after what Quintus showed him the second day, he was less interested in hanging around with Quintus. On the one hand, he believed Quintus was a good man. So he couldn't understand how Quintus could think that what was happening to the rowers was a good thing. By the last day, they spent very little time together. Joshua asked his father about what he had seen.

"Daddy, I saw some men downstairs who were chained and had to row. They looked very unhappy. Some looked at Quintus like they hated him . . . and me. Is it right to treat people like that?"

"No, Joshua. Adonai does not want people to be treated like that," Joseph assured him. "The Roman government often use slaves until they die. Then they use others. Some day Adonai will act to free all the slaves."

"Do our people have slaves?" asked Joshua.

"Yes. Some Jews have slaves. Long ago, when the people of Israel would have a war, they might capture the enemy and make them slaves rather than killing them. But they were not treated like the slaves you saw. Most were treated very well. They lived very simply in those days. They had very few belongings and moved from place to place. People who move from place to place are called 'nomads.' "

"I know, father," broke in Joshua. "That was during the time of Abraham, Isaac, Ishmael, Jacob and Esau, and Moses."

"That's right. But later, when they settled in the land of Canaan, they began to raise crops and build houses. Many of them produced more food than they needed, so some moved off their farms into villages and did other things. Some made sandals. Others made weapons and tools. Others were like us. They made furniture and saddles for camels and donkeys. Others became like Chaim and bought what others raised and sold it in the markets.

"And life became more complicated. Some people were not so successful. They would borrow money and not be able to repay. So they sold themselves as slaves to the person to whom they owed the money. But they were slaves for a limited time. After a few years, they paid their debt with their labor and they were free to go back home to their family. In fact, many of them still lived with their own family, but had to go and work for their master during the day. Most were treated well, but knowing human nature, I am sure there were some of our people who treated slaves badly. That's why there are laws in the Torah that require just treatment of slaves." Joseph wondered if he were going into too much detail.

"But that kind of slavery is okay, isn't it, father? I mean, that is fair, isn't it?" asked Joshua.

"Yes. I believe it's fair, as long as they are treated well."

"I wish we could do something about the slaves below deck," Joshua wished out loud.

"I do too, Joshua," agreed Joseph.

Then Joshua spied some seagulls, his mind distracted away from the topic. He ran to the railing to see if he could see land. None was in sight. He looked for a long time. Then he remembered his little brother. Miriam put a cotton pallet down on the deck and Joshua spent the next hour playing with Jacob and making him laugh.

Arrival in Caesarea

Caesarea was a noisy, bustling seaport city with a long history. During Phoenician times, in the fourth century BCE, Abdashtart, king of Sidon, established it as a small fortified town called Strabo's Tower. The Roman general, Pompey, appropriated it for the Syrian province of Rome in 63 BCE. Mark Antony had given it to Cleopatra, whom Joshua had heard was extremely beautiful.

After Antony and Cleopatra were defeated by Octavian at the battle of Actium in 31 BCE, he gave the city to Herod the Great. Herod built it into a magnificent city and renamed it Caesarea Maritima (Caesarea-on-the-Sea) in honor of the new emperor, who by then had the name Caesar Augustus. Herod also built a hippodrome for chariot races, an amphitheater, a sewage system, palaces, temples, and spacious streets. The inner harbor was dug into the land for mooring ships and warehouses were constructed on the harbor.

Upon Archelaus' removal as king of Judea in 6 CE, Caesarea became the capital of the Roman province of Judea and the official home of the Roman prefect. It was also headquarters for the Roman legions stationed in the province of Syria.

Joseph was anxious to see this exciting city. He had hoped to see the sights in the great city of Alexandria when they changed ships. But they had spent just a few hours there--a disappointment. So he had planned to spend a couple of days in Caesarea to see the sights. The captain of the ship, Paulus Lisius, had at various times over the five-day trip, struck up conversations with Joseph. As they were about to moor their ship, he informed Joseph of a warehouse on the wharf where he could store his belongings inexpensively. Upon arrival, the first thing Joseph was to find some day laborers who unloaded the family's belongings and took them to the warehouse.

Quintus Meridius told Joseph where there were inns along the harbor, but suggested that they not stay there. It was a "rough area," according to Quintus. But he knew of a Jewish inn near the heart of the city.

They found the accommodations very pleasant. Joshua wanted to see the sights. Joseph did too. So the next day they explored Caesarea. One place they found particularly interesting was the hippodrome where they saw the chariot races. The winner was an aristocrat from Jerusalem named Judah ben Hur. Unlike many Jewish men of the time, Joseph did not leave Miriam behind. By the end of the day, they were all exhausted.

The next day, Joseph rented two donkey-carts, loaded them, and headed for Nazareth, accompanied by the fifteen-year-old son of the merchant who rented them the donkeys and carts. It was about thirty-two miles to Nazareth.

They went through Samaria, which always made Jews a bit uneasy. They made sure they had enough food for two days. They were safer being accompanied by Cassius Vitalus, son of a Roman citizen. But the trip was uneventful and when they arrived, a celebration ensued.

CHAPTER 9
JOSHUA'S EDUCATION CONTINUES

Nazareth – A Whole New World

Judeans did not hate Galileans like they did Samaritans, but considered them to be ignorant, brawling hicks, who spoke with a hillbilly Aramaic accent. After the Exile of the Northern Kingdom of Israel in 722 BCE, few Jews were left in the region called Magidu, later know as Galilee. Babylonians were offered land to immigrate to Magidu. The few Jews left there intermarried and lost their hereditary religion. Galilee became known as *Gelil hagoyim*, "district of the Gentiles," by the Judeans. A hundred fifty years before Joshua's time, they were reunited with Judaea by King Alexander Jannaeus. They were forced to either adopt the Jewish religion or leave. Jewish families were offered free land to immigrate.

Galilee was a very fertile region, especially the plains of Asochis and Esdraelon. Agricultural products in Galilee were wheat, barley, dates, grapes, walnuts, figs, and olives.

Joseph and Miriam were glad to be home. The first day they stayed with Joseph's brother, Ishmael. The next day, Joseph found a place to live. It took three days to make the modifications needed to add a carpenter's shop. Like most houses, Joshua's home in Nazareth was mud brick. In the wall by the entrance was a small wooden box containing a parchment with the words of the *shema* from Deuteronomy:

"Hear, O Israel: Yahweh our God is one Yahweh; and you shall love Yahweh your God with all your heart, and with all your soul, and with all your might. . . . And you shall write them on the doorposts of your house and on your gate."

Sandals were taken off upon entering the house. The main part was one room twelve feet square, a bit larger than most local houses. The carpenter's shop was an open area attached to the house, with a canopy over it. The floor of the shop was hardened dirt; the floor of the house was limestone slabs. There was a raised platform, eighteen inches high, where food was prepared and the family could eat and sleep without intrusion by the animals that often roamed freely. The ceiling was ten feet high.

The roof, covered with clay and waddle, was supported by heavy beams that in turn, supported several cross beams. On the side of the house were stairs leading to the roof. There were four beams which held up a canopy over the roof, so that they could have shade when they socialized and cover when they slept on the roof on hot nights. It was also used for drying fruit, flax, and the family wash. Miriam did much of her weaving on the roof. They often ate on the roof. It was usually cooler there.

Usually, only wealthier families could afford divans to recline on, which doubled as a chair for the dining table and a bed. But Joseph, being a carpenter, made his own. The children slept on straw mats. The table was on four legs just a few inches high. Miriam cooked on a small clay stove fueled by charcoal. The windows were small, but larger than most and had wooden shutters. The room was lit by a small, clay oil lamp, fueled with olive oil, which burned day and night. It was too difficult to restart a fire that had gone out. *Proverbs* says a good wife never lets her lamp go out at night. It not only started the cooking fire, but was considered a deterrent for thieves and evil spirits.

When they arrived in Nazareth in 3 CE, Joshua found something new. He had a fairly large extended family, consisting of uncles, aunts, and several cousins. Although he had enjoyed Tanis, there was now a new dimension to his life. Life seemed more secure among family. And they were so glad to see him. Since he was the oldest of Joseph's sons, he got the most attention. But now he also had another little brother. He was now bigger than he was when Jacob was a baby, so it was easier to carry little Joseph.

Children's Education

In the contemporary Jewish society, like most near eastern countries, the mother had primary responsibility for the early education of the children. But when the boy was six or seven, the father took over. He began teaching his son the Hebrew traditions and taking the boy to the synagogue to study the Torah under a rabbi. But the boy was not bound by the laws of Torah until he was thirteen, about the time he entered puberty. He also learned to read and write at the synagogue school, using the Torah as a text.

Boys were supposed to be ready to marry at about eighteen, girls when they reach puberty, at twelve or thirteen, usually marrying someone closely related to them. Once the bride's father and the suitor's representative agreed on the bride-price, the betrothal was celebrated. Betrothal may last a year or more. When they came together, the feasting lasted for a week. On the wedding night, careful examination was made to determine that the woman was a virgin. If the young man died during the betrothal period, she was considered to be a widow.

As Joshua grew, other events began to affect his life and future. On one occasion, he and some boys were playing. Not far from where they were playing, some other boys were gathering wood. Finding a partridge's nest, one of the boys reached in and was bit by a snake.

His friends were carrying him home and came by where Joshua and his friends were playing. Fortunately, his arm was hanging below the level of his heart, slowing down the circulation of the poison. When Joshua heard what happened, he had them put the cot down, and despite the danger to himself, sucked the poison out of the snakebite and saved the boy's life. Then he and his friends found the snake and killed it. The boy was deathly sick for about ten days, but finally recovered.

Then there was the day when Joshua experienced prejudice. It was on the occasion when he and some other boys were playing on a housetop. One of the boys, a Roman named Zeniunus, fell off the roof, hitting his head and seemed to be dead. The boy's parents, who were prejudiced against Jews, immediately blamed Joshua, accusing him of pushing Zeniunus off the roof. But Joshua, who had a healing manner about him even as a boy, gave the comatose boy pulmonary resuscitation and revived him. To assure the parents, Joshua asked Zeniunus, "Were you pushed off the roof?"

"No! I stumbled and fell myself," Zeniunus responded.

The parents were embarrassed by their false accusation, but their prejudice would not allow them apologize to Joshua. Joshua and Zeniunus continued to be friends and play together. The parents did not like it, but their embarrassment over the false accusation prevented them from discouraging their son from playing with Joshua. The friendship between the Jew and the Gentile steadily grew until Zeniunus moved away.

The Jewish Religious Development

The Jewish religion is considered to have begun with the migration of Terah and his sons, Abram and Nahor (about 1900 BCE), from Ur of the Chaldees in southern Mesopotamia, near the Persian Gulf. Terah led his family to Haran on the upper Euphrates River. Their reason for leaving was the invasion of the Amorites, making them refugees.

After his father died, Abram had a dream in which Yahweh came to him, telling him to leave Haran. The dream may have been influenced by the fact that the Hurrian tribes from the north had become more aggressive, forcing them to leave on peril of their lives. So Abram migrated southwest along the Fertile Crescent into the Land of Canaan. In Ur and Haran they had worshipped the local gods like everyone else. But in Abram's dream the God Yahweh gave him a new name, Abraham, said he would become the father of a great nation, and that he would be blessed in order to be a blessing to the world. His son Isaac and grandson Jacob (Israel) carried on the tradition.

Drought drove Jacob (who had been given a new name, "Israel") and his family into Egypt in about 1600 BCE. Although he didn't know it, his son Joseph had previously been sold by his brothers as a slave to Ishmaelites, who had in turn sold him in Egypt. Joseph had risen to the level of vizier (secretary of state and secretary of domestic affairs) under a Hyksos Pharaoh. After the native Egyptians overthrew the Hyksos, the descendents of Israel, who had taken the side of the Hyksos in the conflict, were enslaved by the Egyptians. The oppression became unbearable. The final travesty occurred when the pharaoh decided to have every Israelite boy baby killed at birth. One of the boys escaped death and was eventually adopted by the pharaoh's daughter. His name was Moses. Although he grew up in the pharaoh's household, he had compassion for the enslaved Israelites. Moses rose to the level of vizier under Pharaoh Seti I (1302-1290 BCE). But when he killed an Egyptian taskmaster who was beating an Israelite slave, he was forced to escape to the land of Midian.

Upon returning, Moses asked Pharaoh to allow the Israelites a three-day journey into the desert to sacrifice to Yahweh. Fearing a plot to escape from Egypt Pharaoh refused. Ten plagues then hit Egypt, beginning in September, when a blood red bloom of algae contaminated the estuary of the Nile Delta, producing toxins that killed fish and animals. The "red tide" required extended hours of daylight, warm temperatures, and the nutrient-rich water that was left after the Blue Nile deposited its melted snow in the delta. The decaying fish polluted the waters, forcing frogs ashore. Not finding enough insects, there was mass frog starvation. The dead fish and frogs brought the October swarm of midges (gnats), whose larvae live on microorganisms in decaying animals, followed by the stable fly that makes painful bites in the skin, leaving open wounds, or boils. Also, the African horse sickness, transmitted by a midge killed the livestock.

In February, hail injured humans, animals, and fields of flax and barley. In late February, an infestation of desert locusts which laid their eggs in the wet ground left by the hail wracked Egypt. The ninth plague was darkness from a sandstorm called a *khamsin*, common in Egypt in early March, lasting three days.

The tenth plague was death of the firstborn Egyptian boys. The crops that were not destroyed by hail or consumed by locusts, were contaminated with locust feces and wet grain that molded in warm weather and poor circulation caused by the accumulated sand at the entrance of the granaries for at least three days.

The first to be fed the contaminated grain were the Egyptians' pride and joy, the firstborn sons, who received a double portion. The desperate Egyptians gave grain next to the emaciated firstborn cattle to provide sacrifices for propitiating their gods to end the plagues and save their nation. The priests required well-fed animals for sacrifices, which they ate later. The fear of the Egyptian gods was so great that they fed the firstborn male cattle before feeding others in the family. The first born ate the contaminated grain and died quickly. Others ate grain what was left. They were less susceptible to poison, eating dryer grain below the surface.

The Israelite firstborn of livestock were in no danger of dying because they were sacrificed to Yahweh (Ex. 13:2; Deut. 15:19-20; Num. 18:17-18). Israelites lived in a separate location in the land of Goshen, not affected by the red tide and therefore were sheltered from the related plagues, including the tenth. The hail was localized and did not affect their area. Finally, they lived far enough away from the desert that much of the sandstorm had dissipated by the time it reached them.

They celebrated a sacrificial meal, painting the blood of the sacrificial lamb on the doorposts of their homes. Upon seeing the bloody marking, it was said that the "angel of death passed over their homes." The Israelite boys were spared.

The ten plagues convinced Pharaoh that the Israelites were bad luck. In 1290 BCE, they escaped from Egypt and under the leadership of Moses, the Israelites wandered in the Sinai Desert for forty years. During that time, Moses, as vizier a man used to dealing with legal issues, codified the laws that were the beginning of the Torah that was seen as given by their God, Yahweh. The Torah also placed an emphasis on impurity, focusing on semen, menstrual blood, childbirth, blood, impure animals, and dead bodies. One had to wash after contact with impurity. Later, when they settled in Canaan and more water was available, some also washed their hands before prayer and before or after meals.

The laws codified by Moses also emphasized justice. Many of the laws were not new, but were now codified. There was also an emphasis under Moses that had not existed before in any other culture. In those days, people of other tribes were considered of no intrinsic value. If your tribe was stronger than another, it was considered appropriate to treat them any way you wanted.

But Moses pointed out that Israel knew what it was like to be treated like dirt. That was not the way Yahweh wanted them to treat the stranger in their midst. Aliens were to be protected. So their religion was not based on just pleasing a god so that he or she would bless their local crops or herds. The law of their God had a strong ethical dimension. Yahweh also required charity toward the poor.

In addition, the Jewish God claimed to love all people, not just the Jews. That was not at all common for local patron gods of that time. Sometime later, there was even consideration given toward enemies in war. It was forbidden for soldiers to cut down their enemies' food-bearing trees, a common practice for other tribes and nations.

The focus of their worship during their wanderings was the Tabernacle, a tent in which Yahweh was supposed to have dwelt. When they reentered the Land of Canaan under the leadership of Joshua (1250 BCE), the Tabernacle was located at different places at different times. The Twelve Tribes were an amphictyony in which their twelve tribes were loosely united by their common God (1200-1025 BCE).

When one of the twelve tribes was attacked by a foreign enemy, such as the Philistines, the Edomites, Moabites or the Ammonites, the other Israelite tribes were called on for help. But as the Israelite tribes grew numerically, kinship ties with the other tribes weakened. Sometimes they came to help when called and sometimes they didn't. A deliverer, or "judge," would arise to the occasion and lead in throwing off the aggressor.

This was also a time of great moral laxity. Toward the end of the period, they were led by a circuit-riding priest named Samuel, who acquiesced to their desire to have a king and anointed a member of the tribe of Benjamin, Saul, in 1025 BCE.

When he did not measure up, David (1005-965 BCE) of the tribe of Judah led them; and despite his short-comings, became their ideal of what a king should be. David made Jerusalem his capital, built a palace, and established a fledgling bureaucracy. His son, Solomon, established a full-fledged internationally-connected kingdom, built a temple to replace the Tabernacle, and taxed his people into poverty as Samuel had predicted that kings would do.

Israelite tradition required males to attend three festivals a year at the Tabernacle, and later, at the Temple. During that time, laws and history that had previously been passed down orally began to be written down.

After the death of David's son, Solomon, the kingdom split into two kingdoms. The southern kingdom made up of the tribes of Judah and part of Benjamin, took the name Judah, and followed the Davidic dynasty. The northern kingdom, calling itself Israel, was made up of the other tribes and was ruled by whomever had the most power or could assassinate his predecessor.

In 722 BCE, the northern kingdom was destroyed by the Assyrians under Shalmaneser and Sargon II, and the population was exiled to prevent an insurrection and lost their identity. But the Assyrians were defeated by the Babylonians. In 586 BCE Judah was destroyed by Nebuchadnezzar of Babylonia and most of its surviving inhabitants were exiled, leaving the land practically depopulated.

The people of Judah, who became known as Jews, began to collect their writings, to add to them in light of contemporary circumstances, and to give them greater significance. During the Exile, with the destruction of the temple, a new institution, the synagogue, developed, in which Jews worshipped and focused on the teaching of the prophets. Under the Persian King Cyrus II, in 538 BCE they were allowed to return to their land and rebuild Jerusalem and the temple. Since many had made their homes in foreign lands, especially Egypt and Mesopotamia, not many returned.

It became impossible for many Jews to attend the temple. But they worshiped first thing in the morning and last thing at night in their homes. If there were as many as ten men in a village, most Jewish communities had a synagogue at which they could worship on the Sabbath, and where men could study the Torah, instruct young boys in the Torah, and socialize. All literate Jews were able to read the Torah and the illiterate Jews heard it read and discussed by rabbis and their disciples each Sabbath in the synagogue. Following Ezra, a cadre of Torah scholars arose who interpreted the Torah for their fellow Jews.

Joshua's Rabbi

Not long after they returned to Nazareth, Joshua's formal education began. His first schoolmaster was a rabbi named Zacchaeus. He had already learned his Aleph-Bet-Gimels from his parents. Rabbi Zacchaeus taught him mathematics, reading Hebrew and Greek, and the interpretation of Jewish writings. He was allowed to read any book of the Hebrew writings except the *Song of Songs* scroll. It was considered too racy for young boys to read, which of course, meant he really wanted to read it.

Joshua still spoke mostly Aramaic at home. But he spoke Aramaic, Hebrew and some Greek in Rabbi Zacchaeus' school. He avoided reading the Septuagint, except the books that were not in the Hebrew writings.

The Septuagint was a third-century BCE Greek translation of the Hebrew Torah, Prophets, and Writings. Ptolemy II Philadelphus (283-247 BCE), pharaoh of Egypt, wanted to have the greatest library in the world. He had over two hundred thousand volumes in the Great Library of Alexandria. Ptolemy wanted the sacred Jewish writings in his library. Aristeas, an Alexandrian Jew, proposed that they needed to be translated into Greek. King Ptolemy proposed the project to Eleazar the High Priest, who was so grateful for the project that he offered sacrifices for Ptolemy and Queen Arsinoe, his sister-wife.

The *Letter of Aristeas* says that seventy-two Jewish scholars translated the Torah. Philo says that the translators were sent to separate rooms for seventy-two days and all came out with identical translations. That is how the Septuagint got its name and is designated by the Roman numeral LXX (seventy).

The Septuagint also later included other books that were written over the next two centuries, including *First Maccabees*, *Ecclesiasticus* (also called *Wisdom of Jesus ben Sirach*), and longer versions of *Daniel*, *Jeremiah*, and *Esther*. Others, originally written in Greek, were added like the *Wisdom of Solomon* and *2 Maccabees*. Writings of the period, like *Enoch, Jubilees*, and *The Testaments of the Twelve Patriarchs*, were not accepted and are known as *pseudepigrapha* (false writings).

The Septuagint was extremely valuable for the Jews. Most Jews in the Hellenistic world spoke Greek, the *lingua franca* of the empire, were losing their Hebrew, and could not read the Jewish sacred writings or understand when they were read to them. So the LXX was read in the synagogues outside of Judea and Galilee, and in some instances even there. Joshua especially liked reading the Maccabee rebellion. He pictured himself as Mattathias of Modein, standing up to the persecutors of the Jews and leading the rebellion against Antiochus.

CHAPTER 10
RABBINICAL INFLUENCE

The Teachings of Rabbi Philo
    Like almost all Jewish boys, Joshua had great respect for his rabbi. When he was about twenty-two, Rabbi Zacchaeus thought that Joshua was mentally capable of understanding the teachings of Philo of Alexandria. Joshua learned from Rabbi Zacchaeus that one should listen to a new idea with an open mind. He said that if you only listen to ideas you already agree with, you never learn anything new, you remain stagnant.
    Julius Philo Judaeus of Alexandria (20 BCE--50 CE) was born and lived in Alexandria, Egypt. His father received Roman citizenship from Gaius Julius Caesar. So Philo was also a Roman citizen. His family had high-level ties to the Hasmonean priests, the Herodians, and the Roman Julio-Claudian dynasty. Of course, as an Alexandrian scholar, Philo had a multi-cultural education--Egyptian, Jewish, Greek, and Roman. Like many Alexandrian Jews, Philo did not learn Hebrew well, so he read the Septuagint.
    Philo was famous for using allegory to harmonize Jewish writings with Greek philosophy. He taught that the soul is inflamed by irrational impulses, is corrupted, and can never be satisfied. Like Adam and Eve, the soul of humans perverts the truth and opposes Yahweh.
    Philo also said that the way we treat people, takes precedence over teaching and ceremonial practice. He taught that the fundamental virtue was goodness; from which proceeds prudence, courage, self-control, and justice. Joshua considered the ultimate purpose of the Torah to be justice. He knew it would take a great deal of both self-control and courage to be able to do Yahweh's will.

Philo taught that man cannot reach virtue by himself. It must be implanted by Yahweh. Joshua had, since he was twelve, seen Yahweh as his father, one he could depend on. So Philo's emphasis on total dependence on Yahweh was compatible with Joshua's understanding of the relationship between us and Yahweh.

Rabbi Zacchaeus was well-versed in the teachings of Philo. He saw Joshua's potential and hoped he would adopt Philo's teachings. Philo's philosophy was a means of defending Jewish religious truths to the Gentile world. Influenced by Plato and Pythagoras, he taught a dualistic contrast between God (Greek: *Theos*) and the world (Greek: *kosmos*). He pictured *Theos* as the first cause, emanating divine reason from Himself to the world. His teaching about creation was Platonic, the world having no beginning or end, and time only beginning with the creation of the world.

Joshua could not accept the idea that the world had no beginning because the very first words of *Bereshith* (Genesis) says, "In the *beginning* God created the heavens and the earth" and "When Yahweh God made the earth and the heavens . . . ." Both texts speak of a beginning of the world.

Philo taught that the Greek philosophical term *Logos* (word, reason) was the equivalent to the Hebrew *dabar Yahweh,* "word of the LORD." He considered the Logos to be the medium of Creation, because Yahweh cannot come into direct contact with matter, personally creating only the soul of anything that is good. Joshua did not accept the idea that Yahweh could not come into contact with matter. *Bereshith* said that Yahweh formed Adam out of the dust and took a rib from Adam to make Eve. In fact, he saw the "ruach (Spirit) Yahweh," that created the world, as being the same as Yahweh.

Philo taught that the body was the source of all evil, like the Platonic teaching that *nous* (mind) is a divine emanation from the Essence of *Theos*. He regarded the physical nature of man as defective.

Regarding moral development, Philo taught that before time the condition of the soul was without body, without sex, and morally perfect. Beginning with time, the soul lost its purity and became confined in a contaminated body.

Joshua did not accept that teaching either, because *Bereshith* says, "Yahweh God formed the man from the dust of the ground and breathed into his nostrils the breath of life, and the man became a living being." God also repeatedly said that everything he created was "good."

According to Philo, the first human was morally neutral. But as soon as he met woman, he was trapped by desire and inflamed by irrational impulses, resulting in moral death.

Joshua also rejected Philo's understanding of basic human nature, because *Bereshith* taught that Yahweh had personally made the man's and woman's bodies. And the physical beings, Adam and Eve, were sinless in the beginning. Nor did he believe that the body itself was the source of evil. He believed that evil came from the heart, what Philo called the *nous* (mind). Furthermore, he noticed that *Bereshith* (Genesis) did *not* say that man fell from grace when he met the woman, but that the woman was first tempted by the serpent and then the man was tempted.

Philo saw Moses as *Theos'* means of revelation, which he sometimes communicated through writers like the prophets. Although Philo distinguished between the words uttered by Yahweh and the edicts of Moses, he believed that everything in the Torah was of divine origin, even the letters and accents. He also said that the prophets were extensions of Moses' teaching.

Joshua did not see the prophets as merely extensions of Moses, but as directly speaking for Yahweh. Besides, the prophets did not always agree with Moses. For example, they had different ideas about divorce. While Moses did not concern himself with the end of the world, many of the prophets did. And the prophets did not agree with each other on a number of things, such as whether to marry Gentile women, whether Gentiles would be saved, and what the messianic age would be like.

Joshua believed that Rabbi Philo's teaching on the nature of the Hebrew sacred writings was inconsistent, such as when he said that some teachings of Moses were not of the level of the Torah itself; on the other hand, he said that even the letters and accents were divine.

Joshua's mother had pointed out inconsistencies and contradictory teachings, so how could the contradictions both be true? He believed that all of the teachings should be interpreted in light of the great commandments, "love Yahweh with all your heart and your neighbor as yourself."

Following the methods of Plato, Philo tried to harmonize the Hebrew sacred writings and Greek philosophy by allegorizing the sacred writings. He based his principle of interpretation on a belief in a twofold meaning in the writings, the literal sense for the uneducated and the allegorical sense which could be understood only by the gnostic* initiated. Joshua was very suspect of Philo's allegorizing interpretation, believing that the allegorizing method could enable one to make the sacred writings say whatever the interpreter wanted them to say.

For Joshua, much of Rabbi Philo's teaching sounded too pedantic. As much as he respected his own Rabbi Zachaeus, Joshua could not concur with his rabbi's high regard for Philo's teaching.

Rabbi Hillel

There was another major rabbi of the time, with whom Joshua had some direct contact when he was nine or ten. Hillel bar Gamaliel was born to a wealthy family in Babylonia, perhaps around 60 BCE. His activity in Jerusalem covered the period 30 BCE to 10 CE, when he died.

He was descended from the Tribe of Benjamin on his father's side, and Judah, family of David, on his mother's side. Although his family was rich, he came to Jerusalem to study under rabbis Shemaiah and Avtalion, the "great Scripture expositors," without the financial support of his family. The reason for his family's lack

---

* The idea that only the initiated who had superior knowledge understood God's revelation."

of support is unknown. He supported himself as a woodcutter and lived in such poverty that he was sometimes unable to pay his tuition to study. The esteem with which the rabbis held him was illustrated by the fact that they abolished the fee for his benefit. As head of the Sanhedrin, he was recognized as the highest authority among the scribes of Jerusalem.

Rabbi Hillel's rulings was known for teaching the "spirit of the Torah" and the flexibility of his interpretation of the Torah, whereas Rabbi Shammai was known for his strict "letter of the law" interpretation and a more literal method of interpreting the Jewish Torah and tradition.

Simeon ben Lakish placed Hillel, who taught in Hebrew, Aramaic, and the Babylonian language, on the level of the great Rabbi Ezra, who wrote the *Ezra* scroll. Joshua was inclined to think that Hillel was actually superior to Ezra in that Ezra had treated Gentile women as no more than worthless property.

Rabbi Hillel's Morality and Teachings

Hillel was known for his love for people and his patience. It could be that Hillel's teaching was superior because of his emphasis on self-reflection, which was manifested in his saying, "If I am not for myself, then who will be for me? And if I am only for myself, then what am I? And if not now, when?" It was good rabbinical teaching, cryptic enough to cause one to mull over the meaning of the expression. And his humility is expressed in his paradoxical statement, "My humility is my exaltation; my exaltation is my humility." Another rabbinical expression that begs for reflection.

Hillel was famous for his *Pruzbul* decision, which modified the law of the Year of Jubilees canceling debts in the Sabbatical year. His amendment insured the repayment of loans, protecting the creditor against the loss of property, and the needy against being refused loans for fear of non-payment.

Joshua had learned from his parents that love of neighbor was the way to love Yahweh. His personal contact with Hillel in Jerusalem reinforced their teaching.

Hillel also showed his concern for the poor by both what he said and did. He lived what he taught: the practice of *tzedakah* (righteousness), awe of Yahweh, and humility.

And for Hillel, the concept of neighbors extended to Gentiles. In fact, a Gentile is supposed to have asked Shammai and Hillel to explain the summary of the Torah to him while standing on one foot. Shammai dismissed the man. But Hillel offered his most famous saying, "What is hateful to you, do not do to your fellow man: this is the whole Torah; the rest is commentary." Because of Hillel's witness, the man was converted to Judaism.

Joshua was influenced by Hillel's teaching about the poor. Since he was a child, his mother had sung a song to him that focused on Yahweh's love of the poor in the words:

He has scattered those who are proud in their inmost
 thoughts.
He has brought down rulers from their thrones
But has lifted up the humble.
He has filled hungry with good things
But has sent the rich away empty."

Both of his parents had always told him that, although Yahweh loved all people, He had a special concern for the poor. Hillel strengthened Joshua's resolve to care for the poor when he began his ministry.

Joshua was also influenced by Hillel's openness to sharing Judaism with Gentiles. This was consistent with what he had read in prophets like Isaiah. But Hillel's greatest influence on Joshua was his emphasis on the basic purpose of life. Hillel once stood at the gate of Jerusalem and asked people on the way to work, "How much will you earn today?"

One said, "A denarius."

Another said, "Two denarii."

He followed up by asking, "What will you do with the money?"

"We will provide for the necessities of life," they responded.

He followed up again, "Would you not rather come and make the Torah your possession, that you may possess both this and the future world?"

From the doctrine of man's "image of God," Hillel concluded that it is man's duty to care for his own body.

Hillel had said, "Whoever would make a name loses the name; he who increases not his knowledge decreases." As an adult Joshua would paraphrase and change the emphasis, when he said, "He who tries to gain his life will lose it, but whoever loses his life for my sake and the gospel, will gain it."

Hillel was aware of his own short-comings, saying: "Trust not yourself till the day of your death." Joshua loved that kind of humility. It made him feel that he could trust Hillel's motives.

Rabbi Hillel's Hermeneutics

Hillel made a major step in hermeneutics, principles of interpretation, with the "seven rules (*middot*) of Hillel," which defined the principles of interpreting texts. Although they existed before Hillel, he was the first to systemize them and put them to paper. *Halakah*, or interpretation, is an explanation of specific passages of the Torah, using the principles of interpretation.

The first rule says that what applies in a less important case will certainly apply in a more important case. The application of the principle is often introduced by a phrase like "*how much more . . .*" Joshua would use it often in his teaching.

Rule seven says that the explanation of a passage is obtained from the total context, not just isolated statements. It must be considered for an accurate interpretation, enabling one to apply the text to new, real-life situations. Therefore, the sacred writings remain relevant for future generations.

With regard to the remarriage of a woman whose husband is not known to be alive or dead, the view of Hillel was that she can remarry even on the basis of indirect evidence of the husband's death and that only one witness was sufficient evidence. Ordinarily two witnesses were required to verify legal issues. Women had few rights in the Jewish society. But Hillel's decision provided great security for defenseless women.

Rabbi Shammai

Shammai, a native of Judea, was a builder and engineer, known for the strictness of his views. He was dour, quick-tempered, and impatient. Shammai was concerned that if Jews had too much contact with the Romans, the Jewish community would be weakened. So he emphasized separation between Jews and Gentiles. In the incident when a Gentile said he would convert to Judaism if Shammai could teach him the whole Torah in the time that he could stand on one foot, Shammai drove him away with a builder's measuring stick!

Not long after Hillel died in 10 CE, Shammai became president of the Sanhedrin. So his ideas began to prevail briefly. Joshua resisted the teachings of Shammai for the same reasons that Hillel could not accept them.

Rabbi Gamaliel

Hillel's grandson, Gamaliel I bar Simon, a member of the Pharisee party, was the first to be called by the title "Rabban" (our master), rather than the more common title "rabbi" (my teacher). He succeeded to the position of president after Shammai sometime after 30 CE

Following his grandfather, Gamaliel followed a more liberal Pharisaism. After the death of Shammai, Gamaliel's leadership on the Sanhedrin gave Hillel's school renewed influence. His counsel for moderation saved the apostles after Jesus' resurrection (Acts 5).

CHAPTER 11
OTHER INFLUENCES ON JOSHUA

Contact with Greek

In Nazareth there was no on-going Roman presence. Because Nazareth was such a small town, Joseph had to do jobs in other small villages. Scythopolis was a Gentile town not far from Nazareth, located on the site of the ancient Israelite village of Beth Shean, and was the only city of the Roman Decapolis (Ten Cities) west of the Jordan River.

At times a resident of Scythopolis would come to Nazareth and order a job that Joseph could do in Nazareth. After he would make a chair, table, or couch, he would carry it by cart to Scythopolis or the purchaser would pick it up. Delivery meant additional charges.

At times Joseph would have to go to Scythopolis for a larger project like putting in stairs to the roof. In such instances, Joseph may have been gone for several days. As Joshua got older and more skillful, Joseph took him along. Uncle Ishmael would look out for his mother and little brothers and sisters.

Joseph's contacts with Gentiles required him to learn Koine Greek, the *lingua franca* of the time. Although Joseph's family spoke Aramaic at home, Joseph and his sons had to learn Greek in order to do business with the outside world. The more Joshua was exposed to Gentiles, the more Greek he learned—and the more he wanted to use it at home.

As was true of most Jewish women of the time, most of Miriam's outside contact was with other women and smaller children of their own ethnic group. In Nazareth, that was virtually everyone. Therefore, Miriam spoke Aramaic almost entirely when she went to draw water or visit a friend. Her Greek was very rudimentary.

But as Joseph and Joshua began speak Greek at home, Miriam learned a smattering herself.

Aside from attending the yearly festivals, Joseph did not go to Jerusalem very often. Unlike Nazareth, there were Gentiles in Jerusalem, mostly merchants. Like most Jews, Joseph did not go out of his way to meet and talk with Gentiles, but neither did he treat them with hatred or even hold them at a distance. He greeted them when the opportunity presented itself. Now and then he would even engage in conversation with them. Joshua grew up thinking of talking to non-Jews as a given. In fact, he relished the opportunity because it was a chance to sharpen up his Greek. Since virtually everyone who dealt with the non-Jewish public used Greek, that was the language he used. He even knew a few Latin phrases, but in no real sense was he conversant in Latin.

Example of His Parents

He also saw his father negotiate with others. In their culture, no one ever accepted the original price a merchant or artisan quoted. It was considered bad business, even stupid, not to negotiate for as much you could get. It was expected that the customer would never accept the first price or estimate for the job. That too would have been considered stupid. As part of that culture, it was only natural that Joseph would negotiate in the same way.

When asked questions about the quality of the merchandise or work, most people would exaggerate, maybe even lie without batting an eye. However, if asked to swear in the name of the God of Israel, a Jew would never lie. If he had previously lied about the quality of his merchandise or work, he would sheepishly admit that what he had previously said was not quite true, and would try to give some plausible explanation for the "mistake." The other person would never point out that he had lied, but would cooperate in the cover-up to help the liar save face. Everybody understood the game of negotiations.

With Gentiles, however, one could never be sure. For one thing, in many religions, worship of a god had only to do with influencing the god for one's own benefit and had nothing to do with morality. The other problem was that many Gentiles, especially Romans, went through the motions of religion but didn't take the gods seriously. Therefore, they could say anything they wanted in the name of their god.

Joshua had noticed that *his* father never lied. Joseph's reputation became such that no one ever asked him to swear. Joshua was curious and asked Joseph about his unusual practice.

"Adonai has redeemed us. Our circumcision is a constant reminder of that fact. Remember that Adonai told Moses that he had made us a holy nation. He set us aside so that we could be a blessing to others. Now, how can we convince people of the truth of what we say about Adonai if they cannot trust what we say about ordinary things? Always make sure that when you say something, people can assume it is true. Always let your 'yes' be 'yes' and your 'no' be 'no'."

"I will remember, father," responded Joshua. "I will never forget." Afterwards, Joshua went aside and thought about his conversation with Joseph for a long time. He really liked what his father had said. Joshua never forgot.

There were things that made Joshua uneasy, things he needed to talk about with one of his parents. Joseph was not there, so he talked to his mother. He loved the stories about Israel's conquering its foes in *Judges* and *Samuel*. But he didn't like the story of Samuel telling Saul to kill everyone in a city, including the babies and animals.

"Mommy, you and Daddy always tell me that every human life is precious to Adonai."

"Yes," said Miriam nonchalantly.

"Well, why did Samuel tell Saul to kill Amalekite babies and even their sheep and cattle? And why did Adonai get so mad at Saul when he didn't kill them all?"

His question showed a very serious intent. So Miriam responded more seriously. She stopped what she was doing and gave him her full attention.

"Joshua, I don't believe that Adonai wanted him to kill babies," answered Miriam.

"But Samuel said that Adonai wanted Saul to kill the babies. Is that really what Adonai wanted?" pleaded Joshua, hoping that it was not.

"Well, I think that is what Samuel *believed* Adonai wanted. But, frankly, I don't think the God of Israel would do such a thing. Other gods might. But I don't believe our God is like that," answered Miriam.

"Oh," said Joshua. That was all the answer he needed at that point. He was very relieved.

Miriam pursued the issue. "Not all of Adonai's people taught alike. Do you remember that Ezra made the Jewish men get rid of their Gentile wives?"

"Yes," Joshua said, wrinkling his brow.

"Well, your ancestor Boaz married a Gentile, Ruth. And you are descended from her."

"Ooooh, yeah," agreed Jesus. He dragged out the word "ooooh" for emphasis.

"Sometimes people like Ezra emphasize physical purity when they should emphasize purity of heart," Miriam continued.

Joshua nodded slowly and focused his gaze in the distance, concentrating hard on what his mother had said.

After Joshua had gone to bed that night, Miriam told Joseph about the conversation.

"Well, I'll tell you something," responded Joseph. "That story has always bothered me too. I think your answer was the best answer that you could have given. And what makes me particularly happy is the fact that Joshua thinks about such things and comes to us for answers."

"Yes," Miriam agreed. "I just hope his questions don't get any more difficult."

"They will," Joseph smiled. "I can assure you they will."

Miriam gave a deep, almost explosive sigh. "I know. I just hope I can give him good answers."

"You will," he assured her.

"I hope you're right."

"I'm right. I'm always right," Joseph said with a smirk.

Miriam rolled her eyes up in her head. "This is what I have to put up with," she said, holding her hands up as if making a petition to Yahweh. With the hint of a smile, she continued weaving. Joseph betrayed a sheepish grin and returned to what he was doing. That kind of winsome, loving relationship made Joshua feel very secure.

His parents did other things that Joshua noticed. But he didn't always like them at the beginning. For example, early in Joshua's life, Miriam made sure that he picked up his toys and was given praise when he did it without arguing or whining about it. Before long it was automatic. Miriam also made him go with her to get water at the well, before joining Joseph in the carpenter's shop. At the beginning, he carried a small pot. She assured him that he was very helpful to her. The other women at the well commented how "Miriam's little man" was such a big help for her. Joshua would beam with pride at their compliments. He also acquired a sense of responsibility and pride in helping his parents.

Social Development

When Joshua was eight years old, he played with other children making clay animals. His parents were also happy to see his imagination and artistic interests develop. They also noticed that he had quite a bit of talent in making small, clay statues. A century later, in order to bolster the idea that he was not just human but Yahweh in the flesh, anonymous stories were manufactured that said Joshua had actually brought the clay animals to life.

But Joshua still had a lot to learn. As he became old enough to participate in games with other children, conflicts inevitably occurred. He did not want to give in any more than the other children. His parents usually stayed out of the quarrels and let the children settle the quarrels themselves. Whether they thought he was right or wrong, in order to provide guidance in fairness and sharing, later they would ask probing questions about fairness and what was said and done. Joshua had seen his parents' example of sharing with him and with each other. Their behavior made an impression on him.

As time progressed, he began to attempt to evaluate the legitimacy of his peers' points of view. He could be influenced by the opinions of other children, but he could also hear his parents' reasonable voices in his head. He enjoyed the praise and attention of his peers, but learned from his parents not to be controlled by it.

"Never give in on what you know is right, just to get people to like you," his mother often said. He was a very energetic and competitive child. But he also learned to be friendly and relaxed, even in difficult situations. By the time he was twelve, his parents' influence had convinced him that cooperation was usually better than competition. Of greater importance, he learned that the issue of right and wrong was even more important than either competition or cooperation.

A Turning Point in His Religious Life

A turning point came in his life when he was twelve years old. Every year his parents went to Jerusalem for the Feast of the Passover. After the Feast, while his parents were returning home, Joshua stayed behind in Jerusalem. He was almost considered a young man. He had been on his own in Jerusalem many times. Thinking he was in their caravan with some of his friends, Joseph and Miriam traveled for a day before they began to wonder where he was. They looked for him among their relatives and friends, but he was nowhere to be found. No one in the caravan had seen him. When they did not find him, they returned to Jerusalem to look for him. It took them a day to get back. They asked about him among their friends and relatives in Jerusalem. They went to Bethlehem and asked among their relatives. However, they did not find him there. Finally, in desperation, they returned to Jerusalem and saw rabbi Zacchaeus.

"Rabbi," pleaded Miriam. "Have you seen Joshua?"

"Well, yes," responded the rabbi, astonished. "I thought you knew. He has gone to the temple for the last three days. He has been sitting at the feet of the temple rabbis. And I must tell you that he has been asking some of the most astute questions for a twelve-year-old that I have ever heard in all my years of teaching. I pray to Adonai that he will become a rabbi."

They were already feeling a bit relieved but rushed to the temple. As expected, they found him there listening to Rabbi Hillel. Both relieved and agitated, Joseph rushed in, excused himself, and informed the rabbis that it was time for Joshua to go home.

"Of course," exclaimed Hillel. "But having him at my feet has been a delight. We all have been amazed at his understanding and his answers."

When he came outside, his mother was furious. "Son, why have you treated us like this? Your father and I have been anxiously searching for you." She rarely lost her temper, but this seemed to be an appropriate time.

Joshua was a bit offended that they seemed to be treating him like a child. "I'm sorry you worried. I am twelve years old. I can take care of myself. So why were you searching for me?" he asked. "Didn't you know that I had to be in my Father's house?"

"What are you talking about?" Miriam asked, confused but becoming less agitated and a little embarrassed. She knew that he was right. At twelve, boys become men. Then it became inappropriate for a woman to reprimand him. Some Jewish women did reprimand their adult sons, but it was considered a slight breach of etiquette.

"Well, Adonai is the father of us all. I love my father, Joseph, but Adonai is closer to us than anyone. So, Adonai is my true father."

They understood what he said, but were still confused about what he meant. Nevertheless, he went back in, excused himself to the rabbis, returned to Nazareth with them, and resumed his role as obedient son. After that, Miriam would begin to treat him differently.

But all the way back home, he continued to talk about what he had learned from Rabbi Hillel. Rabbi Hillel said this and Rabbi said that. "I think Rabbi Hillel understands the will of Adonai better than anyone I have ever heard or read," he exclaimed.

After a few hours of listening to what Rabbi Hillel said about every issue under the sun, their ears were worn out.

"Joshua, do you suppose you could wait until tomorrow to tell us what else you learned from Rabbi Hillel?"

Joshua looked at her incredulously. In his youthful enthusiasm, he wondered, "How could anyone not want to hear what Rabbi Hillel said?"

Miriam sidled up to Joseph's side and said out of the side of her mouth, just loud enough so Joshua could hear, "We should have left him in Jerusalem. We should let the rabbi adopt him."

Joshua glanced at her and smiled, rolling his eyes back in his head. Miriam shot a sly glance in Joshua's direction just to see his reaction.

"Mother, you're a trouble-maker," Joseph said as he took her hand, then dropped it and put his arm around her as they ambled along.

The next day the discourse began all over. He hadn't told them nearly enough. It went on all day again. They tried to listen, but they were worn out. Miriam began to recall the incidents surrounding his birth. She began to treasure all these things in her heart. And Joshua continued to grow in wisdom and stature, and in favor with Adonai and men.

Over the next two years, Miriam had to other children, Dinah and Martha. Dinah was born when Joshua was thirteen. She was a small, petit girl with dark olive skin and extremely dark eyes. She was shy and beloved by all. Her older brothers doted on her to the point of spoiling. But she took it in stride and grew up to be so well-adjusted and popular that Joseph when she became of marriageable age, regarding suitors, Joseph literally had the pick of the litter.

The next year Martha was born. She was a husky young girl who knew nothing about reserve. She was so assertive, everyone joked that she should have been a boy. It wasn't that she was unattractive. She had long, black beautiful hair that hung in a profusion of curls. She had high cheek bones and large wide eyes that immediately drew one's attention. But when she became of marriageable age, the gossip in the village focused on who would be brave enough to marry such an independent woman. As luck would have it, a suitor came to Joseph whose ego was strong enough to match hers. He did not try to control her, but treated her as an equal. While there was malicious gossip under the guise of joking about Martha's husband, they too, had a very happy marriage.

As in Tanis, wherever Joseph was, Joshua was with him. He continued his interest in carpentry and masonry. He learned to make gates, tables, sieves, saddles, bricks, mortar, and boxes. By the time he was fifteen, Joshua was almost as good as Joseph. Joseph had developed quite a reputation as a carpenter. Now and then, when Joseph had no work to do, he and his two older boys would go to the village square and wait to be hired by farmers in the area. Jacob too was becoming good enough that he could be helpful in the shop. Miriam had another baby, a son whom they named Simon. So it was a joyful year.

In another way the year 10 CE was a very sad year for Joshua. That was the year word came that Rabbi Hillel had died. Joshua could not withhold his tears. He had been able to see Rabbi Hillel seldom, but when he did, he soaked up everything Hillel had to say. There were very few things that Hillel taught with which Joshua quarreled.

His Acquaintance with Death

Joshua also learned by encountering negative things. One of those was death. It was a constant companion in the ancient world.

Many babies died at birth. Mothers often died bearing the babies. Sometimes both mother and baby died. People were sometimes killed because they spoke against the Roman government or their surrogate Jewish leaders. On a couple of occasions, Joshua had seen slaves die from being worked too hard or beaten. People died from accidents. He had also seen the cruel death by crucifixion. Such cruelty made Joshua's blood turn cold. But even that observation of death did not compare with an incident when he was sixteen.

Joseph had cut himself with a saw. He lost a lot of blood. When the wound became infected, Joseph became very ill. It looked like he might die. They prayed a lot for him and put olive oil, myrrh, and wine on the wound. For over a week, Joshua took his father's place in the carpenter's shop. Because his brother Jacob was still young at the time, Joshua had little real help. He had to work longer hours than usual. Finally, Joseph recovered. Both parents told him how proud they were of the way he had filled in for his father. It never occurred to him to do anything else. He assured them he was thankful that he could be of help to his family. He had been so afraid for his father and was so ecstatic over his father's recovery and thankful to Yahweh, he could barely contain his joy.

One day when Joshua was coming home in the evening with Joseph, a boy ran around corner so fast that he ran into Joshua and knocked him down. But the boy bounced off of Joshua and hit his head against the corner of the house, and died. In anguish, Joshua said plaintively, "As you have thrown me down, so you have fallen, never to rise." Joshua suffered a great deal of anguish over the boy's death.

Joshua had his own scrape with death when he was five years old. He and Joseph had been fishing in a channel of the Nile Delta, just outside of Tanis. As they fished, Joshua was sitting on a boulder that had some slime left on it after the rising of the Nile. But it was dry . . . even a little more comfortable than sitting directly on the hard rock. Being a boy, he could not resist the temptation to kick his feet in the water. This irritated Joseph, who wanted to catch fish.

"Son, stop kicking your feet in the water. You're scaring the fish away," he nonchalantly ordered.

Joshua stopped and tried to concentrate on fishing. But the fish were not biting as often as he wanted, so he would forget and begin to kick his feet in the water again. Joseph would tell him to stop again and he would—for a while. This happened several times.

"Boy you're scaring all the fish away. We'll never catch any fish with you kicking in the water." Joseph got tired of telling him to stop, so he moved away from Joshua, around a bend in the channel.

Joshua could no longer see his father. He kept kicking in the water and catching no fish. What he didn't realize, was that it was getting wet under him. Finally, the slime under him got so slippery that Joshua slid off the boulder into the water. He had just been learning how to swim but was not yet comfortable with swimming. The panic caused him to forget everything he had learned about swimming. He struggled and splashed. He could feel his toes touching the mushy bottom. He could feel that his arms were out of the water, but his head was under. He thought of the irony that part of him was out of the water, but he was going to drown. As he gave up all hope of survival, he felt a powerful hand grasp his arm and jerk him up out of the water. Joshua had not been able to see Joseph, but like a good father, Joseph, continued to keep an eye on his son. When he saw Jacob slip into the water, he came running faster than he realized he could run and pulled the boy up out of the water.

Joshua now realized what it was like to be saved. And as young as he was, he realized that his relationship to the person who had saved him was now changed dramatically. For some time thereafter, when he looked at Joseph, there a certain glow, a halo, around Joseph's countenance that he had never seen before. After a time, the glow dissipated. But although the glow dissipated, there was always something different about his relationship to Joseph that had not been there before. In addition, he now had a certain different relationship toward life.

All these events caused him to begin thinking about issues of life and death.

CHAPTER 12

PREPARATION FOR MINISTRY

The Prediction of John

Joshua had a second cousin named John bar Zechariah, whose father was a priest of the Levite tribe, of the priestly division of Abijah. His mother, Elizabeth, was of the tribe of Judah on her father's side, but also had ancestors on her mother's side descended from Aaron, the older brother of Moses. She was an older first cousin of Miriam. Zechariah and Elizabeth lived in Bethlehem so that Zechariah could carry on his priestly activities in Jerusalem. The lower priesthood was divided into twenty-four groups, three hundred serving for a week twice a year. Only priests were allowed to offer sacrifices. They were assisted by a lower order of clergy, the Levites, who were doorkeepers, janitors, maintenance workers, and cantors.

They were supported by tithes, offerings of first-fruits, and the temple tax. As it was not a full-time occupation, lower-level priests also had other jobs, such as professional scribes, who were lawyers and drew up legal documents. It was considered so important that the holiest places in the temple not be defiled that priests were trained as masons so that laymen would not enter the most sacred areas.

Zechariah was the only leatherworker in the tiny village of Bethlehem. He was known by the Bedouin in the area, who sold him hides from their sheep, goats, and cattle. In turn they purchased leather goods from him. Sandals didn't last long, so he had enough work. Zechariah was known by the Bedouin for his honesty. His son, John, was just like him in that respect. He was also like both his parents in that he was devoted to Yahweh. Yet in other ways, he was not like them at all. He had a fiery personality, often speaking before thinking about the implications of his words. As a boy, he had more than a few fights. And he tended to be less than tolerant of human weaknesses.

Zechariah and Elizabeth were upright people, observing all of God's commandments and Torah regulations blamelessly. Nevertheless, for several years, as hard as they tried, they had had no children, because it was supposed that Elizabeth was barren; and they were both well along in years.

Once when Zechariah's division was on duty in the temple, he was chosen by lot, to go into the temple of Yahweh and burn incense. When the time for the burning of incense came, the assembled worshipers were praying outside. Zechariah went into a trance and had a vision of a messenger of Yahweh, standing at the right side of the altar. Even in this state of trance, Zechariah was startled to see an angel and was terrified.

But the angel assured him, "Do not be afraid, Zechariah. Your prayer has been heard. Your wife Elizabeth will give you a son, whom you will name John.

> "He will be a joy and delight to you,
> and many will rejoice because of his birth.
> He will be great in the sight of Yahweh.
> He will never drink wine or other fermented drink.
> He will be filled with the Holy Spirit even from birth.
> He will bring many of the people of Israel back to Yahweh
>   their God.
> And he will go on before Yahweh.
> He will have both the spirit and power of Elijah,
> to turn the hearts of the fathers to their children
> and the disobedient to the wisdom of the righteous
> to prepare the people for Yahweh."

Zechariah asked the angel, "How can I be sure of this? Both my wife and I are old."

The angel answered, "I am Gabriel. I stand in the presence of Yahweh, and have been sent to tell you this good news. And now you will be mute until the day this happens, because you did not believe me."

Meanwhile, the people were waiting for Zechariah and wondering what was going on. Some began to complain.

"I must get back to my pottery shop," one man groused.

"I have someone coming to pick up a set of expensive jewelry. I can't be late in delivering it," another complained. Others had similar complaints.

But when Zechariah came out, he could not speak to them. They realized that he had seen a vision because he kept making signs to them, unable to speak. He had had a stroke.

When his time of service was completed, he returned home and made a beeline for his wife. Sure enough, Zechariah got Elizabeth pregnant. Unlike many of his fellow priests, who believed that intercourse was lustful and to be avoided except as necessary for having children, Zechariah openly let his cohorts know that he enjoyed trying to get Elizabeth pregnant. At his advanced age, many of his fellow Jews thought it was shameful that he continued trying. But Zechariah saw love-making as a major gift from Yahweh by which he gave his children pleasure. Therefore, he had none of the ambivalent emotional struggles that many of his cohorts had.

When her pregnancy began showing, Elizabeth remained in seclusion for five months. Not long afterwards, her cousin, Miriam, came to visit her. Miriam too, was pregnant, and had just gotten married.

"Adonai has answered my many prayers," she told Miriam. "He has taken away my disgrace of being childless." She and Zechariah had been concerned not only about disgrace, but about what would happen to them when Zechariah could no longer work. Children were their social security.

Birth of John

Elizabeth gave birth to a son just as Zechariah had seen in his trance. Neighbors and relatives come to congratulate her. Even some who had made fun of her barrenness came to rejoice with her. According to tradition, the boy remained nameless until the eighth day, when he was to be circumcised. It was expected that he would be named Zechariah after his father or grandfather. But Elizabeth said, "No! He is to be called John."

Everyone looked at each other, startled. "But nobody in your family has that name," someone protested.

"I know," Elizabeth replied. "But Zechariah wants him to be called John."

Not being willing to take Elizabeth's word for it, they made signs to his father, to find out what he wanted to name the boy. Since he was unable to speak, he motioned for a writing tablet. To everyone's astonishment, he wrote, "His name is John."

Then his ability to speak returned and he began to praise Yahweh. The neighbors were awe-struck, and throughout the hill country of Judea, the rumor mill was churning out this strange occurrence. Everyone who heard this wondered what kind of child he was going to be.

His father Zechariah was so happy that he was filled with the Holy Spirit and began to sing this prophecy:

"Praise be to Adonai, the God of Israel,
because he has redeemed his people.
He has raised up a horn of salvation for us
in the house of his servant David
as he said through his holy prophets of long ago,
salvation from our enemies
and from the hand of all who hate us
to show mercy to our fathers
and to remember his holy covenant,
the oath he swore to our father Abraham:
to rescue us from the hand of our enemies,
and to enable us to serve him without fear
in holiness and righteousness before him all our days."

Zechariah's words had nothing to do with the birth of his son, but the redemption of Israel. It was typical thinking of pious Jews

of his time. Then he turned his attention to his immediate joy and addressed the baby:
> "And you, my child,
> will be called a prophet of the Most High;
> for you will go on before Adonai
> to prepare the way for him,
> to give his people the knowledge of salvation
> through the forgiveness of their sins,
> because of the tender mercy of our God,
> by which the rising sun will come to us from heaven
> to shine on those living in darkness
> and in the shadow of death,
> to guide our feet into the path of peace."

This too addressed the needs of his people, to be forgiven of their sins against Yahweh, so that their eyes might be opened and they would pursue true *shalom*.

Development of John

John did not disappoint his family. From a very young age, he had been told of the prophecies regarding his birth and his purpose in life. Even as a small child, he took it very seriously. John grew and became strong in spirit. He worked with his father in the leather shop. As they worked they talked about the meaning of being a priest. As a priest, Zechariah tended to focus heavily on ritual purity. So the boy was influenced by that perspective. But he also observed his parents' integrity and picked that up also.

Joshua and John were about six months apart, John being the older. When their families got together, John would always take the lead. Six months difference to young children makes a great difference. John was always developmentally ahead of Joshua. As they became older, they were cognitively and physically much closer. But that difference in age seems psychologically to persist into later years. So Joshua was always tagging along with his older cousin.

They liked to play together. John was stronger and a better athlete. He was a tough young boy. In fact, he was the roughest wrestler in his town. His parents often compared him to the patriarch Esau. They avoided comparing him to Samson for obvious reasons. As both of them had been told from their earliest days that Yahweh had chosen them to have a special mission in life, they often discussed matters of their religion.

John and Joshua had seen each other only a few times as toddlers. They played together some, but were too young to know anything about ideas. Since Joshua was living in Egypt from the time he was almost two until he was about six, they did not see each other during that time. Nevertheless, they made up for the lost time when Joseph and his family returned to Nazareth. Each time Joseph and Miriam went to Jerusalem for the festivals, Joshua and John got together. Joseph and Miriam always stayed two or three extra days so the boys could spend more time together.

Jewish Festivals

The Passover was celebrated in the evening on the fourteenth day of the first month of the Jewish calendar. It was also called the Feast of the Unleavened Bread because only unleavened bread was eaten during the seven days immediately following the Passover, as a reminder that when their ancestors escaped from Egypt, they had to leave so quickly that they had no time to let the bread rise.

Joseph and Miriam also went up to Jerusalem for the Feast of Weeks, which celebrated the beginning of harvest. It was fifty days after the Passover. Finally, each year they went to Jerusalem for the festival called *Rosh Hashanah* (the Feast of Trumpets) which is on the first day Tishri/September, and begins ten days before the *Yom Kippur* (Day of Atonement).

The Day of Atonement was a time of fasting and repentance. It was the most sacred day in the Jewish year, the only day of the year when the high priest entered the holy of holies in the temple. He sacrificed a bull for his sins, a goat for the sins of the people, and sprinkled blood on the mercy seat. Then he took another goat, the "scapegoat," laid his hands on its head, confessed the sins of Israel, and released it into the desert, symbolically sending the sins of the people away into the desert.

The Feast of Tabernacles (also called the Feast of the Ingathering) was held immediately after the Day of Atonement, from the fifteenth through the twenty-second day of Tishri, after the harvest.

Sometimes Joseph and Miriam went up for Purim, the commemoration of the deliverance of the Jews from genocide through the efforts of Esther and Mordecai. It was celebrated on the fourteenth day of Adar (March). Joshua and John discussed how, although Mordecai was a heroic figure in the story, the real heroine was a woman. In their patriarchal culture, the boys thought it was significant that a woman would be a heroic figure. This brought on a discussion of Deborah and her role as spiritual mentor for Barak; and Jael who killed Sisera, the Canaanite general who afflicted Israel; Judith who killed General Holofernes, also saving Israel; and Susanna who was the ultimate example of chastity and devotion to Yahweh.

Invariably the boys would get around to talking about Hannah, and how similar John's mother's situation was to the situation of Hannah. John wondered if he would serve in the temple the same way Samuel had served in the tabernacle at Shiloh under the high priest, Eli. In fact, it became a joke with them. Sometimes, when Joshua would call John, he would smile and answer, "Speak, Adonai. Your servant is listening," just like Samuel had done when he was called a third time by Adonai. They both got a chuckle out of that cryptic, historical allusion to Samuel.

If it was not too very cold, Joseph and Miriam also went to the celebration of Hanukkah, a festival that began on the twenty-fifth day of Kislev (December) and lasted eight days, commemorating the victories of the Maccabee brothers and the cleansing and rededication of the temple in 167 BCE, after three years of defilement during the reign of Antiochus IV Epiphanes. It is also called the Feast of Lights because a candle was lit each day for eight days.

Joshua and John as Boys

As they became older, Joshua's and John's discussions became deeper and more insightful. Like Joshua, John gained a lot of insight from his parents. But John's parents were older and by the time he was fifteen years old, both had died. He worked for about ten more years making leather goods and studying under Rabbi Jehoiakim, a Pharisee. Although Zechariah had been a priest, he had not joined the party of the Sadducees. Neither had John. But he had gotten a priest's perspective from his father. Now he was getting a Pharisee's perspective from the rabbi. There were glaring differences in the way his father understood their expressions of the faith and the way Rabbi Jehoiakim understood them.

Since John had no siblings or children, he finally sold the business and house and left Bethlehem for a community in the desert on the west side of the Dead Sea, called Qumran. The community was inhabited by monks who felt that neither the Sadducees nor Pharisees hewed closely enough to the true Jewish religion. They were known as Essenes. They had an excellent library, of which John took full advantage. When he returned to Jerusalem for the festivals, he and Joshua, got together and discussed what each had learned.

The Qumran Community

The priesthood of the Israelites had been hereditary since the time of Aaron, brother of Moses. Members of the family of Zadok, the priest who anointed Solomon king, had been the family of the high priest for centuries. In the second century BCE, the Hasmoneans had usurped the high priesthood from the Zadokites. When Simon Maccabeus, a Hasmonean, ascended the Jewish throne in 142 BCE, the Zadokite family was deposed and replaced by the Hasmoneans. Some of the displaced aristocratic priests joined what became the Essenes and had withdrawn to Qumran.

The Qumran community was a settlement that lay thirteen miles east of Jerusalem, nine miles south of Jericho, and twenty miles north of Engedi. The Dead Sea was less than a mile east.

The settlement was divided into two blocks. The western block was used for work and economic activities, containing a pottery workshop, and storerooms. The eastern part had a large kitchen, a library, and living area. To the south was a large room that doubled as an assembly hall and cafeteria. There was also a second floor with a scriptorium where they copied manuscripts. They had added a large ritual bath, with steps down into the pool.

The settlement was fed by an aqueduct which brought rainwater from the hillside. A dam was built in the Wadi Qumran, forcing water into a basin, emptied into an aqueduct from a tunnel and down to the settlement. The spring rains provided the cisterns with drinking water and water for the ritual baths. Not long before Herod's reign, in 31 BCE, an earthquake had split the eastern bloc. The few crops in the arid area were fed from the large pool and the cisterns.

Qumran had originally been built in the eighth century BCE as an outpost during the reign of Uzziah, king of Judah. As a young man, Joshua wished he could have lived during those days. They seemed so exotic compared to his world.

Qumran had gone into disuse for a long period of time but was rebuilt during the reign of Alexander Jannaeus (103-76 BCE). Prior to that, a group called *Hasidim* ("pious") had fought with the Maccabees against Antiochus IV Epiphanes. The Hasidim later split into two factions, Pharisees and Essenes, over the meaning of the Torah and temple worship. Many groups believed that things were so bad, not only from the oppression by the Gentiles but from apostasy within Judaism, that Yahweh would not put up with the world the way it was any longer and there would be an imminent end of this world order.

The Essenes were a puritanical community that avoided pleasure. But not all were celibate. Some did marry, but marriage was discouraged. They did not have intercourse during pregnancy, believing that the only reason for it was to propagate children. The founder of the community was Zadok, a priest called by his followers "the Teacher of Righteousness," to whom Yahweh made known his mysteries. He taught that the judgment of the world was at hand, when Yahweh would punish the wicked and reward "the righteous remnant of Israel." In their *Manual of Discipline,* they saw their spiritual escape into the desert as fulfillment of Isaiah's prophecy: "Prepare the way of the Lord, make straight in the desert a highway for our God." They were ushering in the messianic age.

The Essenes were preoccupied with ritual purity, washing several times a day. John took from Qumran significant emphasis on ritual purity and later began to wash (Greek: "baptize") people in the Jordan River who responded to his message. But for John's, all-sufficient one-time washing that reflected repentance, was a radical departing from Qumran tradition.

The Essenes also made copies of the Jewish scriptures and Essene documents like the sect's *Manual of Discipline.* They were relatively democratic, allowing all full members in the assembly to express their thoughts. A council of twelve laymen and three priests made the ultimate decisions.

The Essenes also established a community a couple of miles south at Ain Feshkha, which was fed by fresh water springs, producing reeds and date palms, making year-round farming possible. The group at Ain Feshkha was directly related to Qumran. The two communities worked together sharing their resources. Jericho was a major market for the goods produced at Qumran and Ain Feshkha, such as pottery and date honey. They also contracted to reproduce scrolls of a religious nature.

Disenchantment with the Sadducees

Both John and Joshua had become disenchanted with the Sadducees, who, to their thinking, would compromise anything for political power. The young men were much more sympathetic to the Pharisees because they were so zealous for keeping the Torah. Over time, they began to diverge from the Pharisees also, believing they were too legalistic and self-righteous. The day would come when, although they loved and respected each other, their theology would diverge also. Under the influence of the Essenes, John became more rigid; Joshua became more tolerant.

Development of Jewish Writings

As various writings were produced among the people of Israel, some were increasingly seen as authoritative, but were not seen as a fixed canon. There was not consistent agreement regarding the authority of the writings. Nor was there a concept of a verbally pure version that could not be contradicted. But by Joshua's time, many Jews were beginning to distinguish between writings that they considered absolutely reliable, those of more limited value, and those that were spurious.

CHAPTER 13

INTENSIVE EDUCATION

John at Qumran

John had lived past the two year probation period at Qumran, but he never committed himself to the community. They welcomed John because Zechariah was one of the few institutional priests they respected. They came to have great respect for John also, but could not accept him because they shared in a eucharistic meal that included wine. John could not drink the wine because of his commitment to the Nazirite* vow. On the other hand, John developed some reluctance to joining the community because of their exclusiveness and self-righteousness.

In spite of his misgivings, he stayed with them for nearly ten years without actually joining. He made leather goods; participated in their worship and discussions; and purity rites. But his main focus was the library. After a couple of years, he broached the subject to Joshua. But Joshua remained at home and worked with Joseph. Joshua's parents tried to arrange a marriage for him twice. From the way his Uncle Zechariah raved about sexual love, Joshua was very desirous for the experience. He had a young man's passions and fantasies but could not commit himself to marriage. He kept remembering what his parents had told him about his mission in life. He felt the necessity of remaining free to move in any direction Yahweh might lead him. His commitment to the will of Yahweh was greater than his passions. That is probably the reason his parents allowed him to say "no" to the marriages.

---

* Nazirite were committed to not drinking alcoholic beverages.

Joshua at Qumran

When he was twenty eight, Joseph died. Joshua was oldest sibling. His brothers were well aware of both the prophecies and his leanings as an adult. His sisters, Dinah and Martha, were both already married. Joseph had not gotten rich, but made a good living.

Joshua and his father were very close. Therefore, he suffered great anguish at Joseph's death. But after a few months he made a decision. Since Joshua had other siblings to take care of their mother, he decided to explore the possibilities at Qumran. Joshua took his part of Joseph's estate and moved to the community. The members were glad to welcome a cousin of John. They also appreciated Joshua's skill as a builder. Joshua joined in their worship as completely as he was allowed, considering the limitations they imposed on novices.

Like John, Joshua threw himself completely into the use of the library. Considering Qumran's stridence, Joshua was surprised to find writings which went against the teachings of the community. There were copies of *Tobit* in Hebrew and Aramaic, as well as Greek. *Tobit* was his Rosetta Stone to aid him in improving his ability in the Greek language.

During his reading in the Qumran library, Joshua came across the record of an amazing event that touched him deeply. During the Maccabean rebellion, some compassionate Jews had sold all their remaining property in order to pay for the freedom of those who had been sold into slavery.

He thought, "What a wonderful thing it was for people to sacrifice their possessions for others." They were the paragons of what he thought faithful Jews should be like.

Becoming a Member

A major text of the community was *The Damascus Document*, composed between 100 and 75 BCE. It taught that Yahweh raised up the Teacher of Righteousness to lead them in the way of Yahweh's heart. The Teacher taught that there were three ways of violating righteousness: fornication, wealth, and pollution of the sanctuary, violations hidden until disclosed by Zadok.

The Rule of the Congregation, probably written between 100 and 75 BCE, explained the process of becoming a member of the community. The applicant for membership was examined by a man appointed by the head of the masters, who explained all the ordinances of the community. The applicant's own personal wealth and wages were put at the disposal of the bursar who had supervision of the finances. The applicant's funds were kept in trust until the applicant became a full-fledged member.

To become a full-fledged member of the community, a man had to prove himself. On being admitted to the council of the community, there was a two-year probation period. He was not allowed to touch the sacred food nor participate in the wealth of the community for one year. At the end of one year, his record was reviewed. If it was considered acceptable, he was allowed the second step, participation in the ritual washing. The novice could not touch the sacred drink until he had completed a second year, at which time he was registered as a member. Then he could partake of the sacred food and share the community property. At that time, his money was included in the general treasury of the community. The initiated were required to swear to a "binding oath to turn to the Torah of Moses."

In the *Rule*, the communal meal was presided over by their messiah (anointed one) of Israel and a lay leader. Joshua liked the idea of a communal meal. It was a wonderful sign of unity. The community also had washing rites. The *Rule* says, "he may be sprinkled with water for impurity and sanctify himself with water of cleanness," suggesting a moral purification through the physical washing.

Later in the community's history, the baptismal rite emphasized physical cleanliness and total immersion. It said, "No man shall bathe in dirty water or in an amount too shallow to cover a man." Joshua believed that it would be hard to determine just *how dirty* it should be. And the requirement that it be over a man's head seemed pointless except as a contrast to the washing rites of the Jewish mainstream. Also, it would suggest that the earlier rites of the community were not efficacious.

The Rule also taught an exclusivist doctrine. Joshua was uneasy about the idea of the exclusiveness of the community that equated itself with the *yadah* (congregation) of Israel. The document claimed a division between themselves and the rest of humanity, who would suffer "wrath in the deep darkness of eternal fire." That meant, according to the community, that his Aunt Elizabeth and Uncle Zechariah and his parents, faithful children of Yahweh, would be lost forever. He knew better.

Leadership of the Community

There was a council of the community made up of twelve men and three priests who were "perfect in all that has been revealed of the whole Torah." But the priests had the power: "only the sons of Aaron shall administer judgment and wealth." There was a definite pecking order: "Every one of them shall obey his neighbor, the lesser obeying the greater."

The ranking of the members was first: priests; second: Levites; third sons of Israel, and low men on the totem pole were proselytes. One would expect that in a communal society, unclaimed merchandise or funds would go to the common treasury. But at Qumran, the *Damascus Document* said, "Everything that is found and has no owner shall go to the priests." Joshua saw in that rule that the priests were not so egalitarian. He considered them to be greedy, not unlike so many of the priests who belonged to the party of the Sadducees.

Rules of the Community

The *Damascus Document* had rules for everything. One should not speak any "vain or idle" words. They were punished if they went to sleep during session of the masters, if they left during a session as many as three times without cause, if they exposed their nakedness, or if they gesticulated with the left hand (used for bodily elimination). There were numerous rules that made no sense to Joshua. The community had a plethora of punishments for specific infractions. Depending on the flagrancy of the infraction, punishments ranged from a few hours shunning, to reduction of food ration by one fourth, to total exclusion without the possibility of ever returning.

Purity Laws

Joshua also saw some of the purity laws as being absurd. The *Damascus Document* said that a person who is unclean shall not enter a house of worship. Joshua wondered at the logic of preventing someone from worshiping just because of an accident of nature, such as touching a dead body or, nocturnal emission.

Among the interpretations of the *Halakhic Letter*, the Teacher of Righteousness asserted that a stream of liquid poured from a pure pot into an impure pot makes the original vessel impure because the stream connects the two by touching them at the same time. Joshua thought that such pedantic arguments were silly and interfered with the whole point of the Jewish religion.

Sabbath Laws

Purity laws were somewhat cut-and-dried. But the question of what was working on the Sabbath was not all that clear. Therefore, specific issues had to be addressed by experts in the Torah. Many of the *Damascus Document*'s Sabbath rules came right out of the Pharisees' Traditions of the Elders. On the Sabbath no one was to walk more than a thousand cubits.* A nurse must not take up the sucking child to go out and come in on the Sabbath. To Joshua, some of the rules seemed to be cruel and, therefore, contradictory to the Torah which taught them to love their neighbor.

Another rule said that on the Sabbath one should not help an animal give birth and "if she lets her young fall into a cistern or a

---

* A cubit was about the distance from the nose to the tip of middle finger extended sideways.

ditch, let him not raise it on the Sabbath." Another said that "if any person falls into a place of water . . . let not a man come up by a ladder or rope or instrument." He must lift a person out with only his hands, no matter how strenuous, but allowed to remain there if some instrument must be used, no matter how effortless it might make the job.

"Who cares how you save someone's life?" Joshua soliloquized. "Would Adonai really be angry if you saved a man's life with some instrument and not be angry if you exerted yourself but without an instrument?" Rhetorical question.

On the Sabbath, they should "make no decision in matters of money and gain," should "say nothing about work or labor," should not "walk in the field to do business," should not eat food not already prepared, should "eat nothing lying in the fields," should "not drink except in the camp," shall "not draw water into a vessel," shall "not raise his hand to strike" an animal, shall not "wear soiled garments," shall not bring anything into the house or take anything out of the house, and shall "not open a sealed vessel." Except perhaps for the first three, Joshua believed that few of these requirements had anything to do with the purpose of the Sabbath commandment.

More than that, it said, "No man minding a child shall carry it while going and coming on the Sabbath." Joshua considered this rule to be downright cruel. The rules that said, "No man shall assist a beast to give birth" or "if it should fall into a cistern or pit, he shall not lift it out on the Sabbath," seemed to him to be cruelty to animals and required exceptions to the rules. But on the other hand, he had seen this last rule violated many times, even by Pharisees, who ignored the rule when it was advantageous.

The Apocalyptic Era

The War of the Sons of Light with the Sons of Darkness was an apocalyptic* account of a forty-year war that would take place between the Sons of Light (the Qumran community) and the Sons of Darkness (everyone else). First, there would be a war against the "children of darkness" in Israel for seven years. Wicked Jews would be destroyed and the Ten Tribes of Israel would be restored. Then there would be a war against the *Kittim*, a cryptic word for the Roman Empire that would be annihilated after a war of thirty-three years. Joshua wondered what would be the point of the reestablishment of the Ten Tribes, since they were not part of the Qumran community and would, according to the Qumran logic, also be destroyed.

Gentiles

He particularly liked reading *Tobit,* that said that not only will Jews be saved, but so would people from the ends of the earth.

The Halakhic Letter, written by the "Teacher of Righteousness," condemned the priests in the Jerusalem Temple who allowed Gentile offerings and sacrifices. Joshua wondered why offerings by Gentile proselytes devoted to Yahweh should be rejected. Why should offerings from a pure heart be rejected just because of an accident of birth? His parents had argued that circumcision didn't necessarily make a person better than some Gentiles they knew.

In *Judith*, he read that "Judith also dedicated to God all the possessions of Holofernes* . . . and the canopy that she had taken for herself from his bedchambers she gave as a votive offering." Joshua believed that anything offered to Yahweh from the heart was a blessed offering.

---

* Literature reflecting such dissatisfaction with the present state of the world that it predicts the coming of a radical cosmic transformation, often supernatural, in this world or the world to come, often involving revelations through angels, and usually involving judgment of those causing the present situation. John J. Collins, "Apocalyptic literature," *The Harper Collins Bible Dictionary*, p. 39.

Attitude Toward the Poor

As Joshua read the historical scrolls of the Hebrew writings, he noticed that in nomadic life there was little financial and social difference between the rich and poor. But with their settlement and agricultural economy, differences in the circumstances between the economically prosperous and the poor became much greater. Descendents of Abraham no longer took care of each other the way they had in the past. The prophets took the side of the poor. Amos was the most militant defenders of the poor, condemning the rich for taking advantage of the poor or ignoring the plight of the poor. One of his statements said:

"This is what Yahweh says:
'For three sins of Israel, even for four,
I will not turn back my wrath.
They sell the righteous for silver,
and the needy for a pair of sandals.
They trample on the heads of the poor
as upon the dust of the ground
and deny justice to the oppressed."

It is not that there were no laws protecting the poor. For The *Deuteronomy* scroll says, "When you are harvesting in your field and you overlook a sheath, do not go back to get it. Leave it for the alien, the fatherless and the widow, so that Yahweh your God may bless you in all the work of your hands."

Debts were to be canceled every seven years and Israelites who had to sell themselves into slavery to pay debts were freed after six years. During the Year of Jubilees, all slaves were released, regardless of when they became slaves. Jews were not to charge interest on loans to the poor. If their cloak was given as a pledge, it was to be returned by sunset. But as is true in many societies, the laws were often ignored.

The *Deuteronomy* scroll says, "You shall open wide your hand to your brother, to the needy, and to the poor, in the land." Further, "You shall not wrong or oppress a resident alien, for you were aliens in the land of Egypt. You shall not abuse any widow or orphan. If you do abuse them, when they cry out to me, I will surely heed their cry; my wrath will burn, and I will kill you with the sword, and your wives shall become widows and your children orphans."

Since *Proverbs* was a collection of sayings by many different people, there was no consistent attitude toward the poor. In some Proverbs, poverty was considered the result of laziness, lack of discipline, or love of pleasure, drunkenness, or gluttony--the typical stereotype of the poor by those who want to justify not helping them. On the other hand, other Proverbs defended the rights of the poor. One Proverb said, "Stretch out your hand to the poor, so that your blessing may be complete."

Sirach warned against trusting in wealth: "Do not rely on your wealth, or say, 'I have enough.' " He argued that one cannot count on wealth lasting, so one should not trust in it.

Although most rabbis looked down on the poor and fawned on the rich, some were generous to the poor, and considered charity more important than all the commandments. Sirach even went so far as to say:

"As water extinguishes a blazing fire,
So almsgiving atones for sin."

Sirach also said:

"My child, do not cheat the poor of their living,
and do not keep needy eyes waiting.
Do not grieve the hungry or anger one in need.
Do not add to the troubles of the desperate,
or delay giving to the needy."

He even spoke stronger language about depriving the needy:
"The bread of the needy is the life of the poor;
whoever deprives them of it is a murderer.
To take away a neighbor's living is to commit murder;
to deprive an employee of wages is to shed blood."

Joshua also believed that Tobit had his priorities straight when he wrote, "Prayer and fasting is good, but better than both is almsgiving with righteousness."

However, Joshua believed Tobit went too far when he wrote, "Almsgiving delivers from death and keeps you from going into the Darkness" and "almsgiving saves from death and purges away every sin." Joshua saw almsgiving as an expression of a relationship that already existed with Yahweh.

Like Tobit, ben Sirach believed one could be saved by giving to the poor:
> "As water extinguishes a blazing fire,
> so almsgiving atones for sin."

Joshua did not see almsgiving as atoning for sin, but as a way of doing what Yahweh wanted *because* of his relationship to Yahweh.

Ben Sirach seemed to have had an ambivalent attitude toward the rich. On the one hand, he encouraged hard work to get rich and enjoy his riches: "One becomes rich," he said, "through diligence and self-denial."

On the other hand, he expected the rich to exploit the poor, something of which he did not approve: "A rich person exploits you if you can be of use to him, but if you are in need he will abandon you,"

And again, he affirmed:
> "Wild asses in the wilderness are the prey of lions.
> Likewise the poor are feeding grounds for the rich,"

Regarding the rich, he was clear on the tendency of men to never be satisfied with what they have, when he wrote:
> "The eye of the greedy person is not satisfied with his share;
> greedy injustice withers the soul."

Yet he warns the rich man about squandering his wealth:
> "Do not revel in great luxury,
> Or you may become impoverished by its expense."

Joshua did like the Qumran community's commitment to the disenfranchised. The *Damascus Document* said, "At least two days wages every month shall be given to orphans, support the poor and the needy, the wanderer, the virgin who has no redeemer, and for the slave."

On the other hand, another *Mystery Text* asserted that God's people should not humiliate themselves with one of a lower status, such as the blind, deaf, unrighteous, or one who hates. His parents pointed out that there were times when people did suffer because of their sin, people like Saul, Absalom, Haman, Ahab and Jezebel, and the people of Sodom and Gomorrah. His parents also pointed to deaf and blind people who were more righteous, than others who had no such maladies. So they taught him that suffering could be, but was not necessarily related to a person's character.

Teachings About the Messiah

The document called *Melchizedek* focused on the Hasmoneans as prototypes of the priest-king who would be the messiah who would combine both anointed offices. He would bring about the final deliverance of Israel from its sin and lead in the destruction of the wicked. Deliverance would be accomplished through a Day-of-Atonement-type sacrifice by the heavenly high priest Melchizedek.

The *Testimonia* provided scriptural quotations connected to a messianic figure. From it, Joshua thought the idea that there were three messiahs--a prophet, a king and a priest--was clearly taught. He wondered whether these were separate people or just one person. Prophets came from various tribes but priests were Levites, and until the Hasmoneans, except for Saul, kings had been from the tribe of Judah.

Family Matters

Joshua read a great deal of what the writings had to say about women. The *Mystery Text* proclaimed the traditional Jewish teaching that a man should rule over the spirit of his wife. Joshua chuckled to himself when he read this. He lived in a patriarchal society in which the wife had almost no rights. He had seen many men who ruled their wives like slaveholders.

He had also seen men who did *not* take advantage of their privileged position, like his father. In fact, Joshua remembered many times when his father deferred to his mother when he obviously wanted something else. Joshua also knew instances in which a wife actually manipulated her husband while maintaining the illusion that he was the power in the family.

Ben Sirach was typical, stereotyping women: "There is no venom worse than a snake's venom," he wrote, "and no anger worse than a woman's wrath," arguing that Eve was responsible for sin entering the world: "From a woman sin has its beginning."

It was clear that the *Genesis* scroll (*Bereshith*), said that "Yahweh created man in his own image, in the image of Yahweh he created him; male and female he created them." Male and female were basically the same in the eyes of Yahweh.

Joshua was offended by the glaring inequality between men and women. If a woman's husband claimed correctly that his wife was not a virgin when he married her, she was put to death. If his claim was wrong, he must pay her two minahs[*] and never divorce her. He had heard the rumors that his mother had been pregnant before she was married. Considering the kind of person she was, he could not imagine her being killed. It also occurred to him that if she had been killed, he would never have been born.

The Temple Scroll required that the king must marry only one woman, who must be Jewish. The only reason Joshua could see for having more than one wife was for protection of women who had no protector.

Ben Sirach expected the same faithfulness in marriage for the man as he did for women. He wrote: "The one who sins against his marriage bed says to himself, 'Who can see me?'"

Regarding children, ben Sirach's seemed to agree with the Proverb that said, "Spare the rod and spoil the child," when he said:

"He who loves his son will whip him often,
so that he may rejoice at the way he turns out."

Neither of his parents had raised him according to ben Sirach's dictum. Spanking was rare and mild, just enough for him to get the

---

[*] Minah (1.26 oz) = 50 shekels

point. They were more inclined to discipline him by keeping him from doing something he enjoyed like playing with his playmates. As he grew older, they explained *why* they wanted him to do something or refrain from something. Their discipline almost always seemed to Joshua to make sense and was certainly always fair.

Repentance and Forgiveness

Joshua was also impressed with ben Sirach's honesty about his condition. He did not believe in trying to cover up one's own sins before Yahweh, for he wrote: "Do not be ashamed to confess your sins," But he also affirmed that one cannot take advantage of Yahweh's grace by saying:
"His mercy is great,
He will forgive the multitude of my sins."
So he liked ben Sirach's admonition:
"Do not reproach one who is turning away from sin;
remember that we all deserve punishment."

Joshua remembered how his father forgave his mother for being pregnant before they were married. He had noticed how both is parents had forgiven each other many times over the years.

Joshua particularly liked a book in the library called *Mysteries,* a wisdom document that said iniquity is not found in just one people but in every nation and that truth is not found in just one nation, but there is some truth in all nations.

The Importance of Dreams

There was one of Ben Sirach's teachings that Joshua could not afford to accept. He said:
"As one who catches at a shadow and pursues the wind,
so is anyone who believes in dreams . . .
From an unclean thing what can be clean?
Unless they are sent by intervention from the Most High,
pay no attention to them."

Considering the role that dreams had played in his birth, he could hardly accept the teaching that dreams were no more than a shadow. The *Genesis* scroll also recorded how Joseph ben Jacob had dreamed about his future, had interpreted the dreams of men in prison with him, and had interpreted the Pharaoh's dreams that resulted in the saving of Egypt. Joshua accepted dreams that were interventions from the Most High. But there was the rub. How does one know when a dream is a divine intervention and when it is simply a figment of one's imagination. And for that matter, what's the difference? Although he had no answer to that thorny issue, he was sure that dreams couldn't be dismissed as cavalierly as ben Sirach had done.

Sin

The Wisdom of Solomon addressed the issue of the origin of sin within a person, portraying it as beginning in the thinking of man, rather than merely an outward act, when he said: "For perverse thoughts separate people from Adonai."

As Joshua read the scrolls in the library and discussed them with John and others, he began to evaluate what he had learned from his parents. He was very satisfied with what they had taught him. But as he read, his thinking about issues of his Jewish faith continued to evolve. It was a continually exhilarating experience for him.

CHAPTER 14

MINISTRY OF JOHN THE BAPTIZER

Baptism of John
It was in the fifteenth year of the reign of Tiberius Caesar; when Pontius Pilate was prefect of Judea, which included Samaria, Judea, and Idumea; Herod Antipas was tetrarch of Galilee, his brother Philip tetrarch of Iturea and Trachonitis, and Lysanias was tetrarch of Abilene. The person considered the legitimate high priest, Annas, the priest considered by most Jews to be the legitimate high priest, had been replaced by his son-in-law, Joseph Caiaphas. John began his ministry in about 29 CE. He was an ascetic. His clothes were made of camel's hair, with a leather belt around his waist. Part of his food was locusts and wild honey. As a Nazirite, he drank no alcoholic beverages. Many people went out to him from Jerusalem, Judea, and the whole region of the Jordan.

In Herod the Great's day, he had simply appointed high priests without regard for tradition, as did his son, Archelaus. When Rome deposed Archelaus, the Roman prefect, a Gentile, appointed the high priest, even more of an offense to Jews than Herod's appointing him. Therefore, the appointees did not have much prestige among the people. Among many there was even resentment of a priest that would accept appointment as high priest by a Gentile.

Judea was ruled directly by the high priest and his council, the Great Sanhedrin in Jerusalem. As long as the Jews were kept under control, the high priest had great local authority. Joseph Caiaphas ruled for seventeen years, ten of which were while Pilate was prefect. This was the situation when John began his ministry.

People came to hear John for a variety of reasons. Some went to hear John because he was the son of Zechariah. After all these years, the rumor mill had still kept the story going about John's birth. Others came because they were just plain curious. His attire and demeanor suggested the second coming of that wild man during the reign of Ahab and Jezebel, Elijah the prophet. Maybe he would rail against Pilate and the Romans. Still others came who were spiritually empty and searching for answers. Some came hoping that John was finally the one to lead a rebellion and actually throw off the yoke of Rome and its surrogates like Herod Antipas.

And then there were the representatives of Herod Antipas. Some came in their soldiers' uniforms. But others came as spies, pretending to be interested in what John had to say. Antipas had maintained the throne partly because of his spy network, which prevented things from getting out of hand. John seemed to be a potential threat to the maintenance of tranquility.

Joshua's Initiation

When Joshua was in his late twenties, John bar Zechariah the Baptizer began preaching along the Lower Jordan River Valley. The Jordan River originates in the Lebanon Mountains and flows directly south. Tributaries of the Jordan include rivers, wadis, and springs at the foot of Mount Hermon as it drops rapidly for thirty miles from the Lebanon Mountains, into the swampy Lake Hula (Lake Somechonitis). As it exits the lake, it drops much more slowly for fifteen miles to the Sea of Galilee (Lake of Gennesaret and the Lake of Tiberias). Several tributaries empty into the Jordan as it meanders slowly through the lush Jordan Valley, a green ribbon lined with reeds and trees, before emptying just south of Jericho into the Lake Asphaltitis (Dead Sea), which has no outlet.

The Jordan has a number of fords where, most of the year, the river can be crossed on foot. John conducted his ministry at Bethabara, east of the Jordan near a ford a few miles above Jericho. He proclaimed the word of Yahweh, preaching a one-time washing of repentance for the forgiveness of sins.

John's called them to *metanoia* (repentance), involving a complete turning around of one's attitude and will, and devotion to Yahweh, which transformed one's behavior toward others.

Many were baptized in the Jordan River. A surprising number of people came to hear him, particularly because of John's harsh language toward them. He assured them that their heredity of which they were so proud, would not stand them in good stead before the judgment seat of Yahweh. He especially attacked the Pharisees and Sadducees who came to hear him, saying, "You brood of vipers! Who warned you to flee from the coming wrath? Produce fruit that reflects your repentance. And do not say to yourselves, 'We are descendents of Abraham.' For I tell you that Adonai can raise up children for Abraham out of these stones. The axe is already at the root of the trees, and every tree that does not produce good fruit will be cut down and thrown into the fire."

His words had a positive affect. Many responded by asking "What should we do then?"

John called upon people to care about the poor: "The man with two tunics should share with him who has none, and the one who has food should do the same."

There were Jewish tariff collectors who came wanting to be baptized. They were particularly aware of their place in the community, because people let them know in no uncertain terms where they stood. Since they collected taxes for a foreign oppressive power, they were considered betrayers of their own people. They may have expected John to say, "Stop taking taxes."

But instead, John instructed, "Don't collect any more than you are required to."

Even Jewish soldiers came to hear John. "And what should we do?" some asked.

"Don't extort money and don't accuse people falsely and be content with your pay," he answered them.

Messianic Expectations

Messianic ferment was in the air to one extent or another from the time of the Babylonian Captivity in 586 BCE. Some had thought the Maccabees might be ushering in the messianic age in

167 BCE. When Simon Maccabeas established the Hasmonean dynasty as both king and priest, some Jews saw the advent of the messianic age. But the dynasty was not messianic in nature. Many of the Jewish kings were no more righteous than foreign rulers. When the dynasty fell apart, Jewish hopes were dashed. Then a Zealot named Judas the Galilean arose in 6 CE when Quirinius was governor of Syria, who was killed and his movement fell apart. But the Zealot movement continued to be a thorn in the flesh of the Romans. And the hope certainly didn't die. So when John came along, some people began to hope again.

The Testaments of the Twelve Patriarchs

Neither John nor Joshua had ever even given the Zealots the slightest consideration. They had early rejected the Sadducees who did not believe in life after death or accept the prophets and were politically duplicitous, ready to sell their souls for political advantage. The Essenes were good people, but too legalistic, arrogantly self-righteous, and apocalyptic. The Pharisees was the most respected religious-political party.

Recently John and Joshua had been exposed to another writing. Both men loved the spirit of the *Testaments of the Twelve Patriarchs,* written between 137 and 107 BCE. The *Testament of Reuben* said that ". . . through love of pleasure sins enter in."

They discussed the fact that they found pleasure in their relation to each other; in work with their parents; in foot-races, wrestling, and playing together as children; in synagogue worship; and in studying the Torah and the Prophets.

They read in the Hebrew Scriptures that Yahweh too got pleasure in many things. But they had also observed people whose main focus in life was pursuit of pleasure, who did not seem to experience true pleasure. Their frantic pursuit even seemed to end up badly for them. At the very least their lives were empty shells that they frantically tried to fill up with something that was always missing. Therefore, John and Joshua concluded that pleasure was not the problem and that the *Testament* was correct when it said that the "love" of pleasure was the problem.

But they both had problems with *The Testament of Reuben*, which said, "For evil are women." Both had mothers whose examples caused them to reject that attitude out of hand. *Reuben* further said that, ". . . the angel of the Lord told me . . . that women are overcome by the spirit of fornication more than men, and in their heart they plot against men."

It was true that as young men they did not have a great deal of contact with the opposite sex. But from what they could see of the men they knew, it was nearly impossible for women to have a greater "spirit of fornication" than men. They knew of Jewish men who went to prostitutes, but they had never heard of a woman doing that. They concluded that Reuben didn't know what he was talking about.

They liked *Testament's* attitude toward Gentiles. "After all," reasoned Joshua, "the promise to Abraham was that he was blessed in order to be a blessing to the world. That includes Gentiles."

And *The Testament of Simeon* claimed that an angel of Yahweh promised that "[Simeon] and Judah shall appear among men, saving every race of men." What interested them were two statements that did not seem to be reconcilable. One was that "Yahweh shall appear on earth, and Himself save men." On the other hand "Yahweh shall raise up from Levi as it was a High Priest, and from Judah as it were a King, Yahweh and man, He shall save all the Gentiles and the race of Israel." At first, they did not see how that could be reconciled.

And *Benjamin* said, "Keep the commandments of Yahweh, until Yahweh shall reveal His salvation to all Gentiles." He wrote that at the end of time "there shall arise in the latter days one beloved of Yahweh, of the tribe of Judah and Levi, a doer of His good pleasure in his mouth, with new knowledge enlightening the Gentiles."

The Testament of Asher said, ". . . the Most High shall visit the earth, coming himself as man . . . He shall save Israel and all the Gentiles."

At first they had no idea how to interpret the idea that Yahweh would raise up a High Priest and King as Yahweh and man. Then it occurred to Joshua that the text must mean that Yahweh comes to humans through other humans. If that is correct, then Yahweh would come to the world through a human being, who would be the savior.

Testaments of the Twelve Patriarchs on the Messianic Age

The *Testaments* also referred to ungodliness and transgression being committed in the "end of the ages against the Savior of the world, Messiah . . ." and at that occasion ". . . the veil of the temple shall be rent." John tended to think it was speaking literally and Joshua saw it as metaphorical, but what the metaphor represented he did not know.

Levi also referred to "the transgressions of the chief priests who shall lay their hands upon the Savior of the world." They knew enough about the political dealings of the chief priests to not be surprised at that possibility. But they wondered in what way they would "lay hands" on the Savior of the world?

At that time in their lives they did not yet know what the expression "he shall again visit you, and in pity shall receive you through faith and water" meant, or what it meant that "The heavens shall be opened . . . with the Father's voice . . . the spirit of understanding and sanctification shall rest upon him in the water."

Later on, John and Joshua would interpret it to apply to Joshua's initiation into his ministry, which would be performed by John himself.

Levi further says that one will arise who will speak to Yahweh as his father: "And his priesthood shall be perfect . . . for the salvation of the world" and "in his priesthood the Gentiles shall be multiplied in knowledge upon the earth, and enlightened through the grace of Yahweh. In his priesthood shall sin come to an end."

The Testament of Benjamin added an idea that sounded like Isaiah 53, when it referred to "the Lamb of God, and Savior of the world, and that a blameless one shall be delivered up for lawless men, and a sinless one shall die for ungodly men in the blood of the covenant, for the salvation of the Gentiles and of Israel." And *The Testament of Joseph* had a similar expression that sounded to them like Isaiah's Suffering Servant.

And ". . . the twelve tribes shall be gathered together there, and all the Gentiles, until the Most High shall send forth His salvation in the visitation of an only-begotten prophet . . . He shall be lifted up on a tree . . . the veil of the temple shall be rent . . . He shall ascend from Hades and shall pass from earth to heaven."

They agreed that the day would come when Yahweh would exercise his salvation on the living and the dead, but they did not understand "the only-begotten prophet" being "lifted up on a tree," for that referred to crucifixion, the Romans' cruel, execution by torture. They both wished that they could be around when that prophecy takes place—except for the crucifixion.

The Twelve Patriarchs on the Commandments

John and Joshua noticed that there were contradictory laws in the Hebrew Scriptures. It was obvious that some commandments were not of life-and-death importance, such as what color the curtains were in the Tabernacle, while others were of ultimate importance, such as the commandment against killing.

They agreed that *The Testament of Issachar* got at the heart of the commandments when it said "love the Lord and your neighbor" and again, "I loved the Lord; likewise also every man with all my heart." And although they realized that such love would be impossible for human beings to keep to perfection, it was obviously what human beings should strive for. *Issachar* had brought together the two most important commandments from the Pentateuch. Although the two commandments on which these statements are based are not in the same place, they capture the essence of what it means to be what Yahweh created humans to be. For them, the entire purpose of the Hebrew sacred writings became clear. And

Hillel's explanation of the Torah while standing on one foot, fell right into place.

The Twelve Patriarchs on Sin

The Testament of Zebulun also cleared up a matter that John and Joshua had been discussing, namely "what is sin?" It said, "I am not conscious that I have sinned all my days, save in thought . . . except the sin of ignorance which I committed against Joseph." At first John did not get it, but Jesus did.

"Look cuz," Joshua said to John with a twinkle and slight smirk. "Zebulun said that he was not *conscious* that he had sinned in ways other than thought. I don't know if he was self-deluded, but over the years, he had obviously sinned in ways other than thought. He was just not *aware* of it."

"Yeah, I see what you mean . . . cuz." John couldn't help repeating the term "cuz" back at Joshua.

"But Zebulun was clear on the fact that he had sinned in his thoughts without actually acting on his impulse. That is where bad behavior begins, in our thoughts, in our heart. You have seen people whose hatred and resentments were just burning them up, but they did not act on it, right?" Jesus asked rhetorically.

"Yes I have. And deep down inside, I realize there was something wrong with that, even though they did not overtly do anything bad," agreed John.

"And finally, he acknowledged that by not standing up for Joseph against his brothers, he was committing a 'sin of cowardice,'" concluded Jesus.

"Yes, he was one of the younger boys. It is bound to have been hard for him to stand up to his older brothers, some of whom already had wives and children, but he should have," agreed John. "And by not doing so, he sinned against Joseph . . . and Adonai," he summed up.

They looked at each other and nodded with satisfaction, while both were soaking up the insights they had just acquired.

It was late. They said their prayers together and lay down to sleep—but neither one could. They both ruminated for over an hour on their new insights. What satisfaction! They finally drifted off. The future would be different.

John the Baptizer Denies Being the Christ
As John was teaching, the leadership in Jerusalem sent priests and Levites to ask him who he was.

"I am John bar Zechariah," he answered.

"That's not what we mean," one replied. "Are you the messiah?"

He vehemently replied, "I am not the messiah."

They asked him, "Then who are you? Are you Elijah?"

"No," he said, "I am not."

"Are you the Prophet?"

"I'm not that either," he answered.

Finally, they said, "Well then, who are you? Give us an answer to take back to those who sent us."

John replied in the words of Isaiah the prophet: "I am the voice of one calling in the desert, 'Make straight the way for the Lord.' "

They realized that he was claiming to be fulfilling a prophetic role. Then a Pharisee asked, "Why then do you baptize if you are not the messiah, nor Elijah, nor the Prophet?"

"I baptize with water," John replied, "but among you stands one who comes after me, the thongs of whose sandals I am not worthy to untie. I baptize you with water. But he will baptize you with the Holy Spirit and with fire." John had a strange, nagging feeling that he could be talking about his cousin.

John the Baptizer expected the end of time and judgment to come very soon and expected that Yahweh would restore the twelve tribes of Israel, establishing a kingdom of both peace and justice. He did not know how, but he believed it could be that Joshua would be the fulfillment of his prophecy. So John *did* claim to be a forerunner of the coming messianic age.

CHAPTER 15

INITIATION FOR THE MINISTRY

Joshua's Baptism by John

When Joshua was in his late twenties, he had gone out to the Jordan several times to hear his cousin, John. During those times they had long discussions regarding their readings and their ideas about the Jewish faith. At some point Joshua felt called to accept John's baptism. On the day he came, John saw him and was delighted.

"Cousin! I am so glad to see you. How long has it been . . . two weeks, three?" asked John.

"Actually, it has been about six weeks. I have been thinking hard about what you said the last time I saw you. I like your idea of a washing that turns one's life around. I want you to baptize me," said Joshua.

"Has it really been that long?" John asked incredulously. "My, how time flies when you're having fun."

But John tried to deter him, protesting, "Really Joshua, I need to be baptized by you, and do you come to me?"

Joshua replied, "No. I want to do it. It's the thing to do to fulfill true righteousness."

John took a deep breath and nodded. "Okay, let's go."

They went into the water. As Jesus bent over, John placed his hands on Joshua's head and offered a prayer from the Psalms. Then he took a horn filled with water and poured it on Joshua's head in the name of Yahweh.

As he came dripping out of the water, he felt the Spirit of Yahweh descending on him as if it were a dove alighting on him. He felt like the very heavens opened and Yahweh was speaking to him as a father, saying, "This is my son, whom I love; with him I am well pleased."

His mind was filled with the *Testament of Levi,* which said, "The heavens shall be opened . . . with the Father's voice . . . the spirit of understanding and sanctification shall rest upon him in the water." Words of *The Testament of Judah* came to him, which said, "And the heavens shall be opened to him, to pour out the spirit, even the blessing of the Holy Father; and He shall pour out the spirit of grace upon you." Joshua felt a sense of purpose more profound than he had ever felt before. The specifics were not clear but the purpose was. John also sensed that something profound was happening.

"Thank you John. This means so much to me," Joshua said, literally glowing.

"It was my pleasure, cousin. I know Adonai has blessed you and has great things in store for you. Would you stay and join me? We could do great things for Adonai together," John urged him.

Joshua thought a minute. He looked directly into John's eyes. "I don't think so right now. I don't know where my life is headed. I need to spend some time thinking and praying. I am going into the desert for a few days to fast and pray. Maybe our Father in heaven will make His will known to me."

Disappointed, John nodded. "Adonai bless you then and give you his shalom."

"Thank you, cousin. I look forward to seeing you again." Joshua left and went back to Nazareth to inform his family of his decision. So he headed north up the King's Highway on the east side of the Jordan River. He made good time, walking thirty miles, arriving at Amathus in late afternoon.

He was the recipient of hospitality from a local merchant, Joshua bar Judah. They discussed, among other things, John the Baptizer, whom his host admired very much. As John's cousin, Joshua was treated with great honor. He was entreated to stay another day—which he did. But on the third day, over the objections of his host, Joshua said he must leave. Arriving in Nazareth in the early evening, he informed his family of his decision. With pride, his mother kissed him.

"Joshua, I know this is the beginning of the fulfillment of the dreams I had about you when you were born. You have been the most committed to the study of the sacred writings of anyone I have known. And your love for the important aspects of the Torah has made me very happy. If he were were still alive, your father would have been so proud."

He was in a hurry to get started. The next day he left home. He pronounced Aaron's benediction on his entire family: "Adonai bless you and keep you, Adonai make his face shine on you and be gracious to you, Adonai lift up his countenance on you and give you shalom," he said with a lump in his throat and mist in his eyes. He gave each a kiss of peace, took his supplies with him, and left. He had no idea what lay ahead.

Destination Desert

It took three days of leisurely walking to get to Jericho. He left Nazareth, traversed through the Valley of Jezreel, passed west of Mount Gilboa, and stayed at Ginaea the first night. The next morning he got an early start and made it as far as Beth-aven where he spent the night. On the following day he got to Jericho by noon. From there he went south, down the verdant Jordan Valley, into the desert, past Qumran, and south of Hyrcania a few miles. He found a place near the Asphaltitis Sea (Dead Sea). There was actually a little shade there, just below a cliff..

In the desert alone between the Judean Hills and the Sea, he spent several days in prayer and meditation. Symbolism was an important aspect of most middle-eastern cultures, including the Jewish culture. Like the children of Israel who spent forty years in the desert, as Moses was forty days on Mount Horeb, Joshua spent forty days in the desert. He took enough water for four days. After four days, he went to the little village of Hyrcania. He ate a meal of bread and honey, got enough water for four days, and returned to the desert. He did this nine times. During that time, because of food deprivation and the heat, Joshua had several hallucinations. In some of them, he experienced the temptation of Satan.

Testing in the Desert

In one, Joshua's stomach was growling from hunger. His hunger was insatiable. The tempter came to him in a hallucination and said, "If you are the son of Yahweh, there is no reason for you to suffer from hunger. Use your power. Tell these stones to become bread and fill your stomach." In his hallucination he heard the tempter say the sacred name, "Yahweh."

Joshua could literally taste bread spread with goat butter and honey. But in his addled mind, a saying of ben Sirach came to him, which said:

"it is not the production of crops that feeds
humankind.
But that your word sustains those who trust in you."

Therefore, he came to himself and answered, "It is written: 'Human beings do not live on bread alone, but on every word that comes from the mouth of Adonai.'" As a good Jew, even in a hallucination, he could not say the sacred name, so he used the substitute term "Adonai."

In another hallucination, the devil took him to the holy city of Jerusalem and had him stand on the highest point of the temple.

"Come now," he taunted, "When you were washed by John, I understand that you could hear Yahweh saying that you were his son and that he was well-pleased with you. If you are the son of Yahweh," he said, "throw yourself down. See those people in the temple courtyard looking up at you? They are waiting for you to prove you are the son of Yahweh. Do that and they will believe in you. Yahweh will take care of you, for remember it is written:

'He will command his angels concerning you,
and they will lift you up in their hands,
so that you will not strike your foot against a stone.'"

In an honor-shame culture like Joshua's, a challenge must be answered or one would lose face. But to accept it would also be a denial of his mission to defend Yahweh's honor.

So Joshua answered, "No! I will not tempt Adonai my God that way, because it is also written: 'Do not put Adonai your God to the test.'"

On another occasion, he felt light-headed and light-bodied. He felt like he was floating as the devil took him to a very high mountain and showed him all the kingdoms of the world and their splendor. It was a thrilling experience. All the nations of the world laid out before him. He did not know how.

"All this I will give you," the tempter said, "if you will bow down and worship me."

Every human being wants people to honor him. Rulers have prestige simply by their position. In the hallucination, he believed that he had the chance to rule the entire earth. Who could turn down an opportunity like that? But personal prestige was not Joshua's mission. He struggled with his human desire to receive human power.

After a life-and-death wrestling with himself, Joshua answered, "Get away from me, Satan! For it is written: 'Worship Adonai your God, and serve him only.'"

Other hallucinations confronted him with temptations. At times he weakened but did not give in. He finally had a vision of the devil, frustrated, leaving him, and angels ministering to him.

Bad News in Hyrcania

At the end of forty days, Joshua went back to Hyrcania, that dates to the time of Moses' protégé, Joshua, about 1300 BCE. John Hyrcanus built a fortification there along the border of the Judean Desert. Herod the Great used it as a prison for his more-fortunate political enemies. It was occupied by about six contubernia of soldiers. A contuberniam was a contingent of eight men who shared a tent in the field. In a barracks they shared a two-room suite.

Ordinarily, a centurion commanded eighty men*. In this case he only commanded almost fifty, assisted by six decani, commanders of the contubernia, plus a contingent of ancillary personnel—quartermaster, cooks, equestrian grooms, slaves, etc. As long as Judea was peaceful according to Roman definition, Hyrcania was ordinarily manned by Jewish soldiers under the authority of the Sanhedrin. There was even a synagogue there. Most of the soldiers were Hellenized and usually spoke Greek, even though it was their second language.

Joshua spent three days there, feasting, resting, and gaining his strength and his mind back. During his stay, he spent considerable time talking to the soldiers improving his Greek. He was becoming quite comfortable with it. Being quite Hellenized, the soldiers called him by the Greek equivalent of his Hebrew name "Joshua," which is "Jesus." It occurred to him that in a world occupied by Greek-speaking Romans and Hellenized Jews, he may have to go by that name.

He talked to them about the usual things. They were all interested in hearing about his life in Tanis. In out-of-the way places like Hyrcania, soldiers tend to be bored and conversation with visitors was a treat. He talked about his life in Nazareth, his stint at Qumran, his time with John the Baptizer, and his time in the desert. They were interested in all of it. Part of it was the boredom. Although they were thoroughly Hellenized, most were still faithful to their religion. Considering Joshua's background, they honored him as a rabbi. He talked considerably about his changing understanding of the Jewish faith and what Yahweh expected of them.

One of the soldiers informed him of something that caused his heart to feel as if it were crushed. After Jesus mentioned his relationship to John, the soldiers raised their eyebrows and glanced back and forth at each other nervously.

---

* A centurion originally commanded ten contubernia, which consisted of ten men. But the contubernia changed to eight men, commanded by a decanus.

"Jesus," one said, "I'm sorry to have to tell you this. I have heard John teach. He is a wonderful teacher—a prophet. He showed me the error of using my position to take advantage of people. But this week, we have heard that John was arrested by Herod Antipas."

As tears began forming in his eyes, Jesus asked, "What was he charged with?"

"I do not know the details," admitted the soldier, "but he had become very outspoken about Antipas' marriage to Herodias."

John had publicly rebuked Herod Antipas because of his recent marriage. He had left his wife, a Nabatean princess, and married his niece, Herodias, who was already the wife of his brother, Philip. It was a promotion for her.

John had been saying to Herod, "It is not lawful for you to steal your brother's wife."

At the instigation of Herodias, Antipas added to his crimes by having John locked up in prison. Herodias nursed a grudge against John and bided her time, waiting for an opportunity to have John killed. She had been frustrated by Herod because he feared John and protected him, knowing him to be a righteous and holy man. The strange thing is that when Herod heard John, he was greatly distressed; yet he liked to listen to him.

Jesus Heads for Home

Having heard the distressing news, with a heavy heart, on the morning of the fourth day, Joshua bid them "shalom" and left Hyrcania. He climbed the road that was so dusty the soldiers called it "talc road." He made the ten-mile upward climb in the Judean hills to Bethlehem. The closer he came to Bethlehem, he higher the altitude and the more pleasant the temperature. He arrived and spent the day and evening with his cousins. He was anxious to get back to Nazareth and begin his ministry.

But middle-eastern hospitality being what it is, he was compelled to stay two more days. Finally, after three days of feasting and conversation, Jesus announced his intention to leave. His cousins made their obligatory request for him to stay another day. The custom of that culture made it uncouth to remain longer than three days unless the host continued to beg the guest to stay. So Jesus thanked them for their hospitality and declined to stay another day. They sensed Jesus' urgent desire to be on his way, so they did not beg.

The trip from Bethlehem to Nazareth was about eighty miles. The first day's journey brought him to Bethel, an ancient city that went back before the time of Abraham, at which time it was called Luz. Jacob may have given the village its present name. Later, on in his return to Bethel, in a dream Jacob received his new name, "Israel." It had become an important center of worship for the northern Kingdom after the united kingdom split. It was now a sleepy little village. Jesus went to the town square, where he was invited to stay the night in the home of a local pottery-maker.

The next morning he continued his journey to the city of Samaria, twenty miles north of Bethel. It was the capital of a third of the Roman province made up of Samaria, Judea, and Iturea. It was bounded on the north by the Jezreel Valley, on the east by the Jordan River, on the west by the ridge made by Mt. Carmel and the Sharon plain, and on the south by the Jerusalem mountains. Jesus was concerned, because he had heard stories about Jewish travelers being waylaid, robbed, and in some instances even killed by Samaritans. But he had no problem of that kind.

Samaria had been taken and occupied by King Josiah of Judah (640-609 BCE) and the Samaritans' ancient temple at Mt. Gerizim was destroyed by him. It was destroyed John Hyrcanus, in 108 BCE. The intense antagonism between Samaritans and Jews dates from these events. It was resettled by his son, Alexander Jannaeus in about 85 BCE. In 63 BCE it was annexed to the Roman province of Syria and later given to Herod Antipas by Caesar Augustus in 30 CE.

When Joshua had a meal at an inn, some people greeted him with a cold stare, but others treated him with a friendly demeanor. The innkeeper treated him with respect and traditional hospitality.

His parents had been right. He remembered his father's discussions with Galileans who had disdain for Samaritans. Many times he had heard Joseph say, "Well, there are Samaritans and there are Samaritans." Some reluctantly accepted Joseph's point and conceded that there might be a few good Samaritans. Others' prejudice would not allow them to budge an inch regarding Samaritans.

After his meal, Jesus continued on another seven miles toward Bemelilis. But it was toward dusk, when he was accosted by four men. He could tell by their headdress that they belonged to a Samaritan tribe. They did not touch him, but surrounded him, used abusive language toward him, and demanded his money. As he was getting his money pouch out, eight horsemen came riding up, a contubernium of Samaritan soldiers. Seven of them chased down the highwaymen, while the decanus rode up to Jesus.

"Are you all right, sir," he asked.

"Thanks to you, I am fine," responded Jesus.

"We have been after this bunch for some time. They have been waylaying many travelers. They are finished with it now," crowed the decanus. The contuberniam brought the four back, bound with ropes.

"Where are you from?" the decanus asked.

"From Nazareth," responded Jesus.

"I am Joshua bar Joseph . . . or Jesus, if you prefer."

"Well, since we caught them in the very act of robbery, we will probably not need you as a witness when they come to trial. But be available if you are called."

"Yes, I will," Jesus assured him.

Since the sun had already set by the time they left, Jesus wrapped his cloak around himself and slept under an olive tree. The basic clothing was a tunic that had holes for the head and both arms. Over the tunic was a loose-fitting cloak, used to sleep in.

Jesus offered a prayer of thanks to Yahweh for the Samaritan soldiers. He also prayed for the repentance of the four robbers. He continued to think about how different Samaritans were from the way they were portrayed by so many Jews. He knew Samaritans felt the same way about Jews. And he realized that no matter what, some Jews did not want to be informed. They were secure in their prejudice. He told himself *his* ministry would not be like that.

The next day he arrived in Nazareth. His arrival was grist for a celebration. "My wayward son is back home," Miriam exulted.

"Yes, mother. I hope to serve as a rabbi here."

Miriam was ecstatic. She could not have known how things would work out. Like any mother, she had visions of her son astounding everyone with this wisdom and eloquence. He would be a successful and important rabbi. Well, after all, she was a mother.

Preliminary Plans

The next day, Jesus borrowed a donkey from his brother Joseph and headed for Capernaum. He traveled first the sixteen miles to Tiberias. Antipas had only recently built Tiberius on the western shore of the Sea of Galilee in 24 CE and made it his new capital city. The city was built partly on a graveyard. Pious Jews avoided it because walking on graves made them ceremonially unclean. Therefore, it attracted mostly Gentiles and relatively impious Jews, who moved there for free houses and land.

Jesus went to the prison to see John. A rough-talking jail guard informed Jesus that he could see John. His accusatory stare at Joshua, made him very uneasy. He couldn't help but wonder if he was being sized up for a similar situation to John's.

John's cell was below ground and had very little light. It was dank, stuffy, and depressing. There was no bed, only a few dirty blankets on the floor. But to his surprise, John was very chipper.

"Apparently, my words are taken more seriously than I thought," John joked with a wry grin.

"I've been worried about you ever since I heard about your arrest," said Jesus with great foreboding in his voice.

"Joshua, don't worry. I am in Adonai's hands. What can hurt me?" he asked rhetorically.

"I admire your courage, John. But what if Herod decides to have you executed? He can do it."

"Then I am still in Adonai's hands," John responded with complete calm.

John's attitude caused a great calm to come over Jesus. John's words gave him a sense of serenity that he would carry with him the rest of his life.

"What about you, cousin? What has developed with you?" John inquired, changing the subject.

"I went into the desert for forty days and . . ."

"You what?" John interrupted. "I thought I was the only one crazy enough to spend time in the desert by myself. So what happened?" John was absolutely lighthearted.

"Well, all my questions are not answered, but I feel called to be a rabbi and . . ."

John broke in again. "Adonai be praised. Everybody seemed to know it but you." John was ecstatic at the news. He almost forgot his own present situation.

"But I don't know . . ." Jesus hesitated. "I don't think it will be a traditional type ministry."

"Join the club," joked John. "Neither is mine."

They both broke out into hilarious belly-laughs.

The guard outside was startled. He never heard such a thing from inside the dungeon cells, except from those so deranged that they had no idea where they were.

The cousins gave each other the kiss of peace and a benediction. Their humor turned to regretful concern. They both feared that they would not see each other again.

Jesus continued his journey. It was another eight miles north along the shores of the Sea of Galilee to Capernaum, a village of fifteen hundred to two thousand people. The Sea of Galilee was a lake about thirteen miles long and eight miles wide at its widest point. Simon bar Jonah and his brother Andrew lived in Capernaum. Jesus had met Simon when he came to hear John preach. He had come several times and he and Jesus had become close friends. Jesus arrived in Capernaum that evening and stayed at Simon's home.

Simon's mother-in-law was in bed with a fever. They told Jesus about her and asked if he could help her. Jesus took her hand, prayed for her, and gave her a mixture of olive oil and honey. Within a couple of hours her fever was gone and she felt good enough to wait on them.

The next day, they shared a meal and talked about John the Baptizer and what a loss his imprisonment was. Simon had developed great hopes for Jesus' future as a rabbi and had told Andrew about Jesus. After spending some time with Jesus, Andrew caught Simon's enthusiasm.

The word about Jesus had gotten around. Many who were demon-possessed were brought to him, and he drove out the spirits when he talked to the people about their lives and Adonai's love and forgiveness. He put their minds at ease and the demons that tormented them left them. He was also able to heal many of the physically sick.

Most people believed that illness and psychotic behavior were caused by demon possession. Exorcism was considered to be a good way of ridding a loved one of the demons. Many exorcists sold their services and others were charlatans. The sick and mentally unbalanced lived at home with their relatives and, in desperation families resorted to exorcists for help with their loved ones. So Jesus' casting out of demons was not unique. Even magicians' "black magic," worked because the cursed person believed it was effective.

Jesus, Andrew, and Simon spent two days eating and discussing their futures. They agreed that if Jesus were to pick up John's mantle, he would need a bit more experience. So on the morning of the fourth day, Jesus rose early and headed back to Nazareth. He arrived exhausted from having traveled straight through. He got a good night's rest and arose the next morning, open to whatever might come. Adonai had something important for him to do. He was certain of it. But he had no idea what it would be. Time would tell. He was on his way home to begin. Adonai would give him direction.

EPILOGUE

The argument over the relative influence of nature and nurture goes on. Nevertheless, there is no question that the influences in our lives have a great deal to do with who we are and help explain our way of thinking and our behavior. Our cultural context even influences what we see. A geologist looking at the Grand Canyon sees something completely different from an artist. An Inuit sees a lot more in snowflakes than a person from Texas. Our background provides our mental constructs. The same is true of Jesus.

The way people are usually taught about Jesus makes him an ethereal, unreal person. Many Christians never progress past their children's Sunday school understanding of Jesus. Like other children, his parents would have been his primary teachers by their words and by their modeling of what a good Jew was like. His parents did not think like modern day Westerners. Their cultural values were thoroughly Oriental, closer to Arabs of our day than Westerners. But since the time of Alexander the Great, some influences of the Greco-Roman world had crept into their culture. But even Greco-Roman thinking of that time was not much like ours. As we think about what Jesus taught, we need to be acutely aware of how different his understanding of the world was compared to ours.

The accumulation of influences affected his teaching. But what was in his heart influenced his teaching. That is the basis of his teaching. And even in different cultures, Jesus' love of people can be exuded and practiced.

Like any other person, the greatest influences on Jesus were his parents. Also, like any other person, much of what he learned was consciously taught. But most was unconsciously *caught*, without either he or his parents being conscious of it. Saying, "Not all people in that ethnic group ar bad," says more than is apparent in the overt words. Covertly, it suggests that *most* in that ethnic group are bad. Children pick up these cues without realizing it. Parents leave indelible ways of looking at the world on their children long before teachers get hold of them. The same was true of Jesus.

But there were other teachers. We do not know who they were. His early formal education was probably received under the local Nazareth rabbi. Some scholars believe that Jesus may have studied at the Essene community of Qumran (the community of the Dead Sea Scrolls). There are some similarities in Jesus' teaching and theirs, but there are also major differences. They had a baptismal type rite. They also had a eucharistic type meal of bread and wine. But contrary to the humility of Jesus, the members of the Qumran community were quite self-righteous. And contrary to the Qumran community, Jesus was open to Gentiles as well as all Jews.

Others believe that John the Baptizer, a cousin of Jesus, may have been a part of that Essene community for a while and that Jesus may have been a disciple of John, but later developed his own theology and ethic.

This book is a novel, not a history. But neither are the Four Gospels. My book is an attempt, based on the Gospels, as well as apocrypha, and pseudepigraphical writings (second century fantasies about Jesus' childhood that are not in the Scriptural canon), historical books about Jesus' life, books on human development, and my own imagination.

As a Christian, I would like to see this book motivate people to go back to the Gospels, to learn what Jesus taught, to take what he taught seriously, to follow his teaching, and thereby make the world a more humane place in which to live. For, after all, faith is not merely cognitive assent to a set of propositions. It is not an ecstatic feeling of "God's presence." It is not keeping a set of laws. It is not regularity at congregational worship. It is a relationship with God that is expressed in doing God's will with regard to God's creation by acting in accordance with the two commandments love God with all your heart and your neighbor as yourself.

David W. Melber

July 2010

BIBLIOGRAPHY

Achtemeier, Paul J. (Gen Ed.). *The HarperCollins Bible Dictionary.* San Francisco: HarperSanFrancisco, 1996.
Barnstone, Willis (Ed.). *The Other Bible: Jewish Pseudepigrapha, Christian Apocrypha, Gnostic Scriptures, Kabbalah, Dead Sea Scrolls.* San Francisco: HarperSanFrancisco, 1984.
Beck, Norman A. *Anti-Roman Cryptograms in the New Testament: Hidden Transcripts of Hope and Liberation* (rev. ed). New York: Peter Lang, 2010.
_____. *Mature Christianity in the 21st Century: The Recognition and Repudiation of the Anti-Jewish Polemic in the New Testament* (Expanded and Revised Edition). The Crossroad Publishing Company, 1994.
Boring, M. Eugene. *The New Interpreters Bible—The Gospel of Matthew* (Vol. VIII). Leander E. Keck (Ed.). Nashville: Abingdon Press, 1995.
Culpepper, R. Alan. *The New Interpreter's Bible—The Gospel of Luke (*Vol., IX). Leander E. Keck (Ed.). Nashville: Abingdon Press, 1995.
Douglas, J. D. *The New Bible Dictionary.* Grand Rapids: W. Eerdmans Publishing Co., 1962.
Davies, Philip R.; George J. Brooke; and Phillip R. Callaway. *The Complete World of The Dead Sea Scrolls.* London: Thames & Hudson, 2002.
Humphreys, Colin J. *The Miracles of Exodus: A Scientist's Discovery of the Extraordinary Natural Causes of the Biblical Stories.* San Francisco: HarperSanFrancisco, 2003.
Josephus. *Antiquities.* Grand Rapids: Kregel Publications, 1963.
Keck, Leander E. *Who is Jesus?: History in the Perfect Tense.* Columbia, S.C., University of South Carolina Press, 2000.
Malina, Bruce J. and Richard L. Rohrbaugh. *Social-Science Commentary on the Synoptic Gospels.* Minneapolis: Fortress Press, 1992.

Metzger, Bruce M. and Roland E. Murphy. *The New Oxford Annotated Bible with the Apocryphal/Deuterocanonical Books—New Revised Standard Version.* New York: Oxford University Press, 1994.

Miller, Maeleine S. and J. Lane Miller. *Harper's Encyclopedia of Bible Life.* Edison, N.J.: Castle Books, 1978.

Packer, J. I., Merrill C. Tenny, and William White, Jr. *The World of the Old Testament.* Nashville: Thomas Nelson Publishers, 1982.

Platt, Rutherford H. Jr. (Ed.). *The Lost Books of the Bible and the Forgotten Books of Eden.* Alpha House, Inc., 1926.

Roberts, J. M. *Ancient History: From the First Civilizations to the Renaissance.* London: Duncan Baird Publishers, 2004.

Sanders, E. P. *The Historical Figure of Jesus.* London: Allen Lane, 1993.

Schrage, Wolfgang. *The Ethics of the New Testament.* (David E. Green, Tr.). Philadelphia: Fortress Press, 1988.

Severy, Merle (Chief). *Everyday Life in Bible Times.* Washington D.C.: National Geographic Society, 1967.

Throckmorton, Burton H., Jr. (Ed.). *Gospel Parallels: A Synopsis of the First Three Gospels.* New York: Thomas Nelson & Sons, 1957.

Wikipedia, Inc.

Wright, George Ernest; Floyd Vivian Filson (Eds.). *The Westminster Historical Atlas to the Bible.* Philadelphia: The Westminster Press, 1945.